Ghost of Sangju
A Memoir of Reconciliation

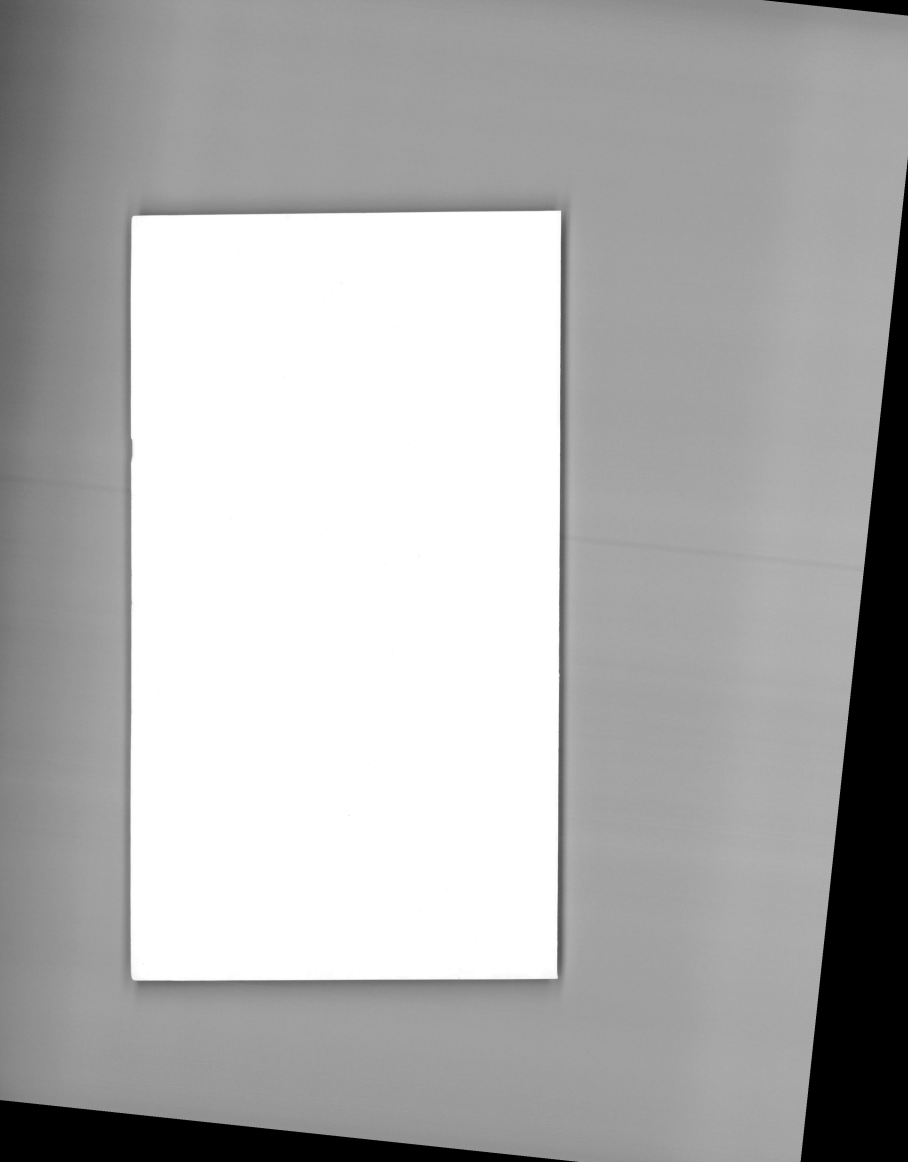

Praise For Ghost of Sangju

Soojung Jo writes with clarity, wisdom, and the bravery required to fully illuminate the human condition. This is a brilliant and cinematic debut, heart-wrenching and triumphant, liberating and expansive. From Kentucky to South Korea, from West Point to parenthood, from anger and grief to healing and joy, this is a vital contribution to adoption and American literature. This is an exciting and beautiful new voice. - **Lee Herrick, author of *Gardening Secrets of the Dead***

Soojung Jo is trying to create an urtext with *Ghost of Sangju*, the urtext of her identity. She is trying to take control of the act of making. The reader has the sense that this is the book Jo has always been writing and always will write, and yet that it is a book she could only have written after reuniting with her Korean family. It is no mistake that I read in these pages the same comparison to the velveteen rabbit made real by love that I myself have expressed as an adoptee parent. This is a narrative that will bring an adoptee to tears, that closes in on the "primal" state Jo is interested in. - **Matthew Salesses, author of *The Hundred-Year Flood***

Soojung shares her truth with authenticity. She employs a razor sharp wit and presents the complex realities of the adoption experience with integrity for herself and those around her. - **April Dinwoodie, Chief Executive, The Donaldson Adoption Institute**

Ghost of Sangju is a book about more than adoption, of course. It's about a basic human need and right: to understand who we truly are. - **Maureen McCauley Evans, Light of Day Stories**

Soojung Jo has a written a book that is honest, riveting, and at points, incredibly heartbreaking. Early on, Jo reveals that as a child, she wasn't sure if she was real or not real; one gets the sense that *Ghost of Sangju* is a testimony, a demonstration to both the world and herself that she is, in fact, extremely real, that her experiences and history are important to chronicle. If decades of literature have hidden adoptee stories such as Jo's from view, with this brave memoir Jo has firmly asserted that her narrative, and others like it, can no longer be ignored. - **Karissa Chen, author of *Of Birds and Lovers*, and *Hyphen Magazine* fiction and poetry editor**

This memoir by Soojung Jo offers a most unique perspective on adoption through the singular lens of a daughter, adoptee, wife, birth mother, and adoptive mother. She finds a way to tell her story with humor, a sharp wit, heartbreaking vulnerability, and unflinching honesty. It's thrilling and necessary to have this beautiful memoir added to the ever growing adoption narrative. - **Randy Reyes, Artist Director, Mu Performing Arts**

Ghost of Sangju should be required reading for all Asian Americans because it is the kind of story that is bigger than just Soojung Jo. It is a story of identity. It speaks to the heart of the struggle for all people of color who live in a country where—just because of the way they look—are considered perpetual foreigners. - **Koji Steven Sakai, Screenwriter/Producer and Vice President of Programs, Japanese American National Museum**

Ghost of Sangju is a valuable contribution to the adoptee-memoir canon, and I recommend that adoption professionals and prospective parents in particular read this book. It might be difficult to read and tempting to discount Soojung and her Omma's story as only one story; it is one story, but it resonates because it is, in fact, many of our stories. It is time that these narratives are honored and validated, so that birth families and adoptees do not have to exist, as Soojun writes, as "a sprit suspended between two worlds and two families, to be forever in between." - **JaeRan Kim, PhD, adoption and child welfare researcher and author of the blog,** *Harlow's Monkey*

Ghost of Sangju
A Memoir of Reconciliation

By
Soojung Jo

Published by,
CQT Media And Publishing, and
Gazillion Strong.

Cover Artwork by Kim Jackson

ISBN-13: 978-09885858-7-4

Table of Contents

For my Omma, and for all the parents and children who were ever separated, who have reunited, and who still search. For every person who has longed to know their history and their blood. As our stories become known, may they illuminate the path that led us here—and close it forever.

Prologue

I was born in South Korea and named Soojung. I was three years old when I arrived in the US to be adopted by an American family and renamed Raina. At twenty-five I gave birth to the first of three children, and at thirty-three I adopted one more from China. I was thirty-six when I learned the identity of my Korean mother, or *Omma*, and thirty-seven when I learned that my Korean father was her kidnapper and rapist.

He had found her at a bus stop and dragged her away to rape and imprison her. He locked her away for several months until she became emotionally, physically, and financially dependent on him. She was out of her mind. She has few memories of that time. Yet, there is one unforgettable and lasting relic of those years in captivity: she gave birth to his daughter.

I'm that daughter, and although we can't speak the same language, I believe she would say that becoming a mother saved her. After a year of raising her baby girl in his basement, subject to his alcoholic beatings, Omma overcame her Stockholm syndrome and decided to leave.

It was as simple as that too—just getting up to leave. He no longer had to physically confine her because she was an uneducated, single, young mother in Korea with no other choice but to stay. But having a child gave Omma resolve, and eventually she left his basement to make her way in a country that had no way for young, single mothers. She quickly found herself homeless and alone— in an impossible situation that we endured for nearly two years. Finally, out of desperation she allowed an orphanage to send me away for adoption.

Omma has had many years to live with her ghosts. In those decades, she could have submitted to hatred of a man, a family, and a society that took so much. She has tasted every flavor of loss, but she never swallowed bitterness. The only reason I know about her story—our story—is because she never sowed those seeds of hate and despair. She chose a better path of hope and forgiveness, and even after thirty years she never stopped looking for her lost daughter.

I believe Omma would say her child saved her because my children also saved me. I spent much of my youth and early adulthood focused on myself—how lost I felt, what I didn't know, what I didn't have. It was my first child, a daughter, who broadened my view, took me outside of myself, and finally rooted me to this world. My next two children, both boys, taught me serenity and joy. My last child, a daughter adopted from China, opened my heart to an awareness that if I stopped acting like an abandoned child, I could become a whole adult.

Because my heart became open, I finally took some small steps to reach out toward my Korean history. Because her heart had not closed, Omma had never stopped reaching for me. Although oceans, nations, and decades stood between us, we somehow found each other.

It was a blow to learn that Omma had never meant for me to be taken from her, and to know how desperately she once tried to get me back. Her revelation about my Korean father, though, was devastating. That knowledge moved a dark, animal part of me. It makes me a little terrified of myself, knowing that his wretched blood flows in my veins. It makes me wonder how so much light and darkness can reside together, and whether it is even possible to have the light without the darkness. It forces me to hold onto something more: that I am saved because I have two mothers and four miraculous children who have taught me all the ways a family can be.

Contact

On March 17, 2013, at 8:13 a.m., I receive the email message that changes everything:

"Hello. I'm jeesoo moon from korea. I tried to contact you but couldn't..so.. if not, so sorry. . Actually my aunt looking for her doughter. Her koran name is soojeung park. I think. ..you are soojeung park. My cousin. . If you are not,, very sorry, this is my cell nb. Now i'm in NJ."

In the seconds it takes to read the words, that email reverses my lifelong path away from my beginnings. It starts the unfolding of a story forty years in the making, from well before my birth, of one woman's quiet fortitude and tenacious hope. The sheer unexpectedness of that message knocks the wind from me.

My first response is suspicion. *How can anyone think this prank is funny? Are they trying to con me? Are they looking for money?* Next, briefly—*Maybe it's not a joke.* I have no intention of becoming a victim, so I contain my small swell of hope.

I shoot back a hurried message, full of demands.

"What is your cousin's birthday? Where did she live in Korea and why was she separated from your aunt?"

Jeesoo's response is almost instant, as if she's sitting at her computer, breath held, praying for a response.

"I'm not sure her birthday..but she is around 38years old I think. She born in seoul of korea n lived. The reason of sepaeated is long story. but my aunt n my mon trying to looking for her after separated. If you want, I can ask my aunt the reason. And she wants miss her doughter."

We go on back and forth for a short while, and then we arrange a phone call for later that evening. I mean business, and clearly Jeesoo does too. I find a Korean-American translator, a friend-of-a-friend named Heidi, who is thrilled to help in this extraordinary circumstance.

Finally the agreed-upon hour arrives and I call Heidi.

I fill her in on the details as I understand them, and we go over the types of questions I want to ask. Then, I conference Jeesoo into the call. Her voice is warm and girlish, and she speaks in the distinct, staccato rhythm of Korean language.

Jeesoo and Heidi jump right into conversation, while all I can do is wait. Although I can't understand the words, I study the sound of Jeesoo's voice for any clues that might indicate our relationship. I listen for family resemblance—can such a thing be heard? Do I hear anxiety in her voice? Relief or desperation? I recognize none of these, for although it was once my first tongue, Korean is now so foreign to my ears that I can't even detect the inflections of her voice. I wait for the translated words.

As the conversation goes on, Heidi doesn't ask me what questions I'd like to ask Jeesoo; they carry on as if I'm not here, and with this great wall of language between us, I might as well not be. Jeesoo delivers long, fast monologues, and Heidi responds in low "mmm, mmm" sounds that convey both sympathy and understanding. Even her sympathetic murmurs sound like Korean.

Then Heidi speaks in English.

"Soojung, this is what happened. Your mother and aunt have been looking for you. She was very young and you were homeless, so she gave you to an orphanage for care. She tried to get you back, but they made her sign papers, and they processed you for adoption. She didn't know where they sent you, so she left her information at the orphanage, hoping you would find her."

Heidi pauses as Jeesoo explains something further, and then she continues.

"Last year your mother and aunt asked your cousins to help look for you. After a year they saw your picture on the adoption website. Jeesoo works in New York, and she sent you the message. She wants you to know they have been looking for you a long time, and they love you very much."

I already know much of this from Jeesoo's email, but hearing the words spoken aloud takes the wind out of me again. I'm aware of being conscious because I can hear her words, and I see the sunlight streaming through my bedroom window, and I feel my own body still attached to the arm that is attached to the hand that is holding the phone. I comprehend Heidi's words telling me history I thought I would never learn, but I can't seem to make a concrete connection with them. It's as if I'm in a parallel universe, peeking through one of the doors of Einstein's dreams and observing another dimension.

This moment feels like a scene from a movie, and I am just an actor portraying the relic of an out grown childhood fantasy. After all, I've been acting through my whole life, so it's easy to resist the many small bubbles of hope floating in my stomach, lungs, and chest. They can't be trusted, so my defense against them is a series of discrediting demands.

"Heidi, I need to know how she got my information. I need her to send me pictures, like photos of me with her aunt. Ask her if the aunt knows anything about me that no one else would know, like birthmarks or personality traits. I need to know what they want from me." I search my mind for more. "And we have to do a DNA test. I won't give any personal information until we do that."

Heidi conveys all this to Jeesoo and then translates her response. "Soojung, she'll ask about photos. She wants you to send her the DNA test instructions. They'll do it. They know you're the baby Soojung they've been looking for. They know," Then Heidi editorializes, "Raina, I think they're being honest. I can tell from Jeesoo's voice that she's telling the truth, and this family will be devastated if it's not you."

With that, the conversation that would change

everything is over.

I report the outcome to my husband Brett as if I am delivering the weather forecast—nothing more personal than the news.

****

My anxiety-fueled search for a DNA test has a few complications. I leave for a weeklong business trip the next day, so I can't use a local lab until after the trip is over. I'm also not sure how we'd get a maternal sample from another continent.

However, I'm persistent and a little desperate, a combination that can yield amazing results. With a bit of research and ingenuity, I find a certified lab called IDENTIGENE that accepts samples from our distant locations, honors overnight parcel service, offers the fastest processing time, and delivers confidential results online. I study the IDENTIGENE informational website. They have high product reviews that range from disturbing ("This is my 4th test and I'm glad to say I'm still not the daddy!" and "I'm so glad I know now which man to take to court!") to inspiring ("My twin and I were adopted and found our parents through social media").

What a strange, delightful world we live in, I think.

IDENTIGENE is certified for court and immigration proceedings, so if they are good enough for the US legal system, I decide they are good enough for me. I zip out to Walgreens and purchase the DNA collection kit. My cheeks burn with embarrassment as I pass the indiscreet box to the young man at the register (Now I know which man to take to court!).

To hell with him, I think as I rush away with the treasured box.

I send Jeesoo instructions to overnight the maternal samples to the lab in Utah. Her aunt (my mother?) must be as eager as I am, because she immediately heads to the hospital to send her sample. Even with the twelve-hour time difference between South Korea and Florida, we get our DNA to the lab by March 19, only two days after first contact. IDENTIGENE promises testing results in two business days. I email the nice lady at IDENTIGENE about every ten minutes for those two business days, and on the third day I receive the email notification that our results are available.

You have never seen a person click through an email, login to a website, and open a file so fast. Almost immediately, the results flash upon the computer screen before me. It takes my eyes and brain a moment to process the large amount of data in the PDF file: report date, case number, certifying scientist, and a listing of all our genetic markers. In the center of the page, boxed in a maroon banner, are the words "Not excluded as the biological mother." Well that seems kind of vague. I click back to the website's "How to Read Your Results" page and scan for the relevant info:

Not excluded = IS the parent.
A CRI over 100 is admissible in court as proof of paternity. Ours is 31,857.
Probability of relationship: 99.99%

*****

I'm still on business travel, alone, apart from my home and family, when I read the report that confirms a mother in Korea still loves me, never stopped missing me, and never stopped looking for me. I swallow my shock and disbelief, moving in pantomime through the rest of the workday. I'm an excellent actor.

In the early evening I leave the office to return to my hotel. As I steer the rented Toyota out of the parking lot, I feel a slow cracking inside me like the breaking of floodwalls. I emit an audible, high-pitched "Oah!" sound · as the force of everything inside erupts from me. The surge grows into wild bursts, and my breathing grows · heavy as small streams strengthen to great waves. Shaking now, I pull the car to the side of the road where I become a full-blown explosion, splintering and shattering from the inside out. The mighty Mississippi breaks forth in my heart, my levees break, and my mind floods.

I have a mother I have a mother I have a mother I come from somewhere I am real I am a person I am loved they never forgot they never walked away I have an omma mommy omma omma I'm not rejected I'm not broken I'm not half unfair so unfair why couldn't I have that why did we have to suffer so much why suffering omma there are people there are my people they know me remember dream omma so heartbroken so unfair how can it be true how did they lose me how did they find me so much lost so much suffering omma

I hunch over in great sobbing spasms, a mess of tears, snot, and heaving cries. My thoughts deteriorate into incoherent blubbering—I am somewhere below, above, and all around thought, somewhere primal and raw. I sit there for a long time like this, with my mind numb but my body an electrical storm of every feeling I had never allowed myself. It all comes out.

*****

Once I have proof of our relationship, the lines of communication break wide open. I am ravenous for photos. I hound Jeesoo for more, more, and more. She never tires of my relentless questions or of translating emails and securing more and more photos. The photos pour in, and they tell so much of the story. For the first time, I see my mother's face—as she looks today, as she looked at my age, and even as she looked when she was just a girl, not long before she became my mother. I see the faces and families of a brother and sister, cousins, aunts, uncles, nieces, and nephews. I have an entire community of family in Korea.

As hungry as I am for photos, I'm even more frantic for answers. Who was my Korean father? What were the circumstances of my birth? Why did they keep me for two years? How did I end up in an orphanage, and why was I sent to the US for adoption while she kept two other children? Only the truth can resolve my dissonance.

At the same time, I experience tremendous confusion about why I even care about these strangers in Korea. It might sound strange to those who have never had to extricate the meaning of family from its corollary, blood, but as an adopted person I had been forced to pull the concepts of family and blood apart at an age when I was just learning what they meant. If the rest of the world defined family by hereditary bonds, then how could I make sense of my own family? Only by rejecting the basic tenant of blood.

I've always watched the families around me with puzzlement: How to explain parents who stand by their children who have committed murder, rape, or worse and still claim to love them...How to understand why we cling to those who hurt us, or chase those who reject or abandon us, when we could never forgive those same behaviors outside of our biological circle...Why such loyalty and primacy? I've never understood this bias toward one's own genetic bonds.

Having a blood family suddenly means revising a definition of family that I have, over many years, learned to accept. How can I hold both concepts in my mind or find room for both families in my heart?

Over the next year, we exchange letters and pictures. I fly to Korea, they fly to the US, and we have a series of introductions and reunions. In May 2014, I receive the letter from my Korean mother that explains the full story. She asks my forgiveness, as though absolution is mine to give. In that letter, the awful and beautiful story of our two intertwined lives and our deep, undeniable connection unfold before me.

Part 1
Reformation

"Ask a cloud: What is your date of birth?
Before you were born, where were you?"

~ Thich Nhat Hanh

Rumors of My Existence

Omma's letter, May 4, 2014

    I was born as the youngest child, with one brother and sister. Twenty-two months after I was born, my mom gave a birth to my younger sister. Then, when I became twenty-nine months old, my mom passed away. A few months later I had a stepmother, but I don't remember that period.

    I was always quiet and played alone with books. I read a lot and was good academically, but I could not study as much as I wanted. When I was in my fifth year of elementary school, my teacher asked the class, "Who will go to middle school after graduation? Raise your hands." When I came home, I asked my father whether I could go to middle school. My father said yes, but my stepmother was so angry about it. The stepmother said, "We don't have any money," and then my father kept quiet. After that, I lost my incentive to study. Accordingly, my grades fell, and when I was in my sixth year of elementary school, my parents could not pay my tuition fee, so I had to quit school.

*****

Autumn 1985

    I've always known I am a myth. Rumors of my existence pervade my childhood, and although I want to believe in my existence, there's little supporting evidence. Sure, I have flesh and bones that seem real to the five senses, but even a young child knows the senses can be fooled.

    I keep score.

    Things that make me real: I have thoughts in my

brain. I can move my eyeballs and see the world around me. When I eat food, it disappears into my belly. I am solid enough for my parents to hold. I can make water swirl by flushing the toilet. Sometimes other people can see me and hear me, and they believe I'm real too.

Things that make me unreal: Real people are born, but I came off an airplane. My mirror face is opposite from my family faces. I have feelings inside my body but they can't come out. Sometimes people can't see me, but sometimes people constantly stare at me. The thoughts in my brain don't sound like the words spoken around me.

The evidence ends in a split decision, so I decide I must be from a fairytale. I adore the lovely tales of magical dark woods where spritely creatures help princes find princesses and sweep them away to safety. If I were a fairy-tale princess, that would explain so many of the real-unreal discrepancies. In fact, I think I'm probably Korean royalty—the daughter of a forbidden romance between the astonishingly beautiful young princess and her one true love, the handsome and brilliant prince of a neighboring kingdom. Their scandalous love magically (and platonically) resulted in a daughter who was more beautiful than her princess mother and also more genius than her princely father. Yes, that's the most likely explanation of why I was never born, because fantasy births are like pure light. To save the kingdom from some terrible thing (or maybe to protect me, like Sleeping Beauty), I was fake-born from an airplane delivery in O'Hare International at the age of three. Someday I'll be called upon to save the whole fantastical kingdom named Korea, and I'll also become a Senator, a best-selling novelist, and an astrophysicist.

In my seven-year-old mind's eye, the kingdom of Korea looks a lot like a real-life Cinderella castle, and my Korean subjects look suspiciously like the white Americans all around me. My Korean kingdom is basically Disney World. I really have no idea where Korea is or why it's any different from Japan, which is in the news a lot.

Because of Japan's prominence on the *NBC Nightly News*, I am about eight years old when I first become aware of being *other*—foreign, outside, separate. Because this lesson comes from my own family, it resonates deeper and truer than playground taunts ever have.

We're all sitting around our brand-new, giant oak dinner table. I'm in love with that massive table—the lion faces carved into the backs of the matching chairs and the miraculous removable leaf that makes the tabletop shrink and grow on demand. Between that enormous table and our new vinyl tile floors, I'm sure we must be rich.

At the head of the dining room, another massive oak structure presides over our meals: The Entertainment Center. In its belly rests our beloved twenty-seven-inch cathode ray tube TV, further evidence of our bourgeoisie success. That TV always plays during dinner—the easier to distract us with. We ruminate over meals of goulash, ham, pork chops, soft canned vegetables, and pineapple-upside-down cake while digesting the evening news. Between complaints about the union stewards and annoying family members, Dad makes comments about the news:*This country's goin' to hell,* and *Dammit everyone's out to git us.* Then Mom answers, *Now Larry, now Larry.*

It's pot roast night, my favorite. I smash sections of soft potatoes and carrots together on my plate, shred a pile of beef on top, garnish it with torn white bread slices, and drizzle the whole mess with gravy. I shovel bites of this concoction into my mouth and watch in fascination as Tom Brokaw reports on a group of Japanese executives touring US factories. I am mesmerized—these people are Asians like me, but they are important in their business suits, stern and unfriendly.

We watch in silence, my parents, my sister, and me. After the segment my dad, a career blue-collar union guy at General Electric, announces with disgust, "They should all go back where they came from."

My chewing slows, the chunks of my pot roast mash feeling gluey all of a sudden. I glance between him and the TV, then him and the TV again. Those businessmen fascinate me because, unlike most people I know in real life, their physical appearance somehow validates mine. Even if I can't understand whether Korea and Japan are different countries or why either might be interested in America, my instincts say that I am somehow just as connected with them as I am to the people at my big fancy dinner table.

It doesn't make any sense that Dad wants them to go where they came from. I feel like I'm as much one of them as I am one of us, although I can't really sort out how this could be true. If I'm one of them, does he want me to go back too? How can I go back if I didn't come from anywhere but a far off fairy-tale kingdom named Korea? Maybe there is no place for half-real people like me. Maybe fairy-tale princesses can only live between worlds.

Mom keeps telling this story for years, though I never understand why. Maybe she wants to make light of her own embarrassment or to distance herself from complicity. Maybe she just thinks it's a funny anecdote— *Your father said they should go back where they came from! He didn't even realize he was talking about you!* I wish she wouldn't tell it because the story gets more humiliating as I get older. It makes me see too clearly everything that is so ignorantly unnatural about my family. My heart breaks every time she tells it, but I know better than to let on.

*****

Mom always says she was born to be a mother. She loves to hold me, and she takes my face into her hands and lists all the ways we are the same—the ways we're just like every mother and daughter. Her deep, singsong voice is the rhythm of rolling Kentucky hills, and in that voice she confides, "You have my brown eyes, see how our eyes are the same? Your hair's only a little darker than mine. I used to have thick hair too, but then I teased it so much in the sixties it got mad and fell out." Even though I knew these are silly lies, I enjoy her attempts at sameness.

I love Mom's stories, and she has plenty of them for me to love. She grew up poor on money but rich on love and happiness, the second oldest of five children in a three-bedroom house in Fairdale, Kentucky. Her mom, my Gran-Gran, was a dainty little woman who had once worked as a model in Louisville to help support her family during the Great Depression. Her father, my Grandaddy, was a towering, Biblical man who had been raised the son of a Baptist preacher and served as a Marine in the Pacific theater during World War II. The two of them embodied the Great American Romance for over fifty years. They took their romance to their graves.

Mom tells me stories of how the family met me and how I adjusted to being their daughter. I think these stories are funny, and it confuses me why parts of them make her look sad.

"Mommy, tell me stories about me."

"Which one do you want to hear?"

"I like the ones about me acting weird. How I hid things."

"Well hon, how 'bout I start before that. How 'bout when we went to the airport to meet you. We were nervous, and Kim was so excited!"

Kim is my sister, a year older than me and adopted from Korea four years before me.

"Oh you know how hyper your sister is. The flight was delayed, and we had to stay in a hotel in Chicago and she was jumping all over the room. And then we went to the airport and she was jumping up and down at the glass where we saw the planes."

"Kim is crazy!" I giggle.

"Yes she was acting really crazy. And then we saw you comin' off the plane. In the pictures they sent us you looked so big, but when we saw you, you was just tiny like a baby even though you were almost three. I thought, *Lord, I didn't bring clothes for a baby!*

"You was scared, but Kim brought two matching dolls and she gave you one. We was driving back from Chicago, and Kim was talking and talking to you. You'd never know y'all didn't speak the same language! That's when we brought you home."

"Now tell me about the dresses and hiding things," I insist.

"Okay, okay. Well you did pretty good but it was so hard for you for awhile. Every night I heard you singin' yourself to sleep in a Korean song and I just knew in my heart that some mom in Korea must have loved you very much. You had nightmares every night for a long time and screamed in Korean words, but we didn't know what they meant. I asked someone who knew Korean, and he said it was um-ma um-ma, the word for mom.

"The first day you was here we put a new dress on you and you was so happy. You just twirled around in that dress and was so proud of yourself. When we tried to change your clothes that night, you hollered and fought. You acted like we wasn't ever gonna give that dress back to you. I figured maybe they didn't give clothes back to you at the orphanage. You did that every night for awhile."

It's funny to think I was such stupid baby.

"Then there was that purse Mamaw gave you. It was

a big black thing, just as big as you were, and Lord, you dragged that purse around everywhere and you put *everything* you liked in that purse. My car keys, bananas, toys, and we always found those dresses in that purse. Every day you filled that bag up, and every night I emptied it back out again."

The story I love most is how her heart was always broken until she became a mommy.

"Oh yes, the only thing I ever wanted to be was a mommy. When I learned that I couldn't have babies like other women, my heart just broke down. But then I found out there was wonderful babies like you and your sister all the way around the world in Korea who needed mommies."

"Why did we need mommies? Didn't we already have some?"

"I don't know hon. For some reason your birth mother couldn't keep you. She was probably really young or poor. But I'm sure she loved you so much. It must have been so hard for her, and she must have loved you so much to give you up for a better life."

I don't understand this—when people love you so much they are willing to get rid of you. I think if I loved someone that much I'd want to stay with them. It doesn't make sense that love would make a mother leave, and I wonder when this mother will love me that much too. I get the idea that love might be something to both desire and fear, and maybe if we don't love each other too much I won't have to go away again. I wonder why love works for everyone else, but it doesn't work for me.

Mom strokes my hair, rubs my back, and goes on, "When your sister came to us, my heart learned how to beat again. *Bomp... bomp... bomp*. Just like that."

She taps her hand against her heart, and I tap my own hand in time with hers.

"Tell me what happened when you got me," I urge.

My favorite parts of her stories are the parts about me.

"Oh, that was the happiest day of my life cause when we got you, our family was complete. I had everything in the world that I ever wanted—two beautiful daughters."

I like that part a lot. It makes me seem so important.

"And then my heart was healed. It finally knew how to beat again. *Ba-bomp… ba-bomp… ba-bomp.*" Again, our two hands, hers large and mine tiny, beat in time against our hearts.

She holds me for awhile longer, still and calm. I love the envelope of her arms—my tall, strong, American mother whose love is so profound it keeps her heart beating, whose protection reaches so far that she could even make my nightmares go away. Inside those moments, it somehow makes sense how a little girl from nowhere could be both myth and real at the same time.

*****

Summer 1986

My family lives in a town called Shepherdsville, Kentucky, which we kids call "Sheeptown" with contempt. It's one of those small towns where three families basically run everything, and everyone knows everyone else. Our neighborhood, Peaceful Valley, is a typical rolling Kentucky suburb made up of several-acre lots that sprawl in the narrow places where the hills meet. Some neighbors have horses, others have small crops. To our left are the crazy neighbors who have one of those giant satellite dishes mounted on the hillside next to our yard. We can always hear a woman calling from their deck, *"Harold! Harold!"* but Harold seems to be avoiding her.

Our house is at the top of an acre lot on a hill. In winters, we ride round disc sleds down that hill in a kamikaze blaze of snowed-in glory. In summers, we substitute the sleds for a red Radio Flyer wagon, using the handle for steering and nothing for brakes. At the bottom of our yard is a productive, quarter acre garden full of cabbages, green beans and squash. Rows of sunflowers stretch their long necks toward the bright, sultry sky. Kim and I run down our hill to pick the sun-warmed cucumbers and tomatoes straight from the vine and eat them like apples. We fill our pockets with fresh blackberries from the garden and feel the juices stream down our legs, as they gets mashed while we slide down our blue aluminum play set. Together, we seek refuge from the summer heat under a great persimmon tree, and in the autumn we slurp its fruits.

At the end of such a summer and the start of a new school year, the fourth grade stretches out before me, exciting, seemingly never-ending. This is the year I will join the drama club and eventually be cast as the pipsqueak Molly in our feature *Annie* production. Later, I'll learn to play my first band instrument—although Mom and Miss Upton will laugh at my first preference, the saxophone, asking who would hold it for me, and then relegate me to the flute. There will be long afternoons at Girl Scouts and two summers at Conservation Camp, but none of this has happened yet. We are still in late August, suffering under the oppression of an Indian summer in the Ohio River Valley.

It's recess, and I'm perched alone at the top of our dome-shaped jungle gym, wondering what friends and adventures might await me during this school year. The sunlight feels like bathwater on my skin, like steam in my lungs. My shorts stick to my legs, and my straight black hair clings to my neck.

"Hey Raina!" I hear a classmate calling me. I turn, in my shyness hoping to make a new friend.

"What happened to your nose? Did you run into a

wall? Is that why it's so flat?" He pushes his nose down with his thumb, turning his hands over upside down to pull the corners of his eyes back. "How come you're a Chink? How did your parents get a Chink baby?"

I hear another boy chanting, "Chinese, Japanese, dirty knees! Hey Chink, do you eat dog?"

There is no friendship in their voices, only taunts that isolate me, push me further into myself. Mind racing. Dodging arrows.

I am not here, no one can see me, I am not real. No one can say things that poke and stab at my fragile nine-year-old heart.

I summon a retort. "Oh yeah? At least my parents picked me! Your parents were just stuck with you! And I'm a Gook, not a Chink. Get your words right dummy head!"

I run to the monkey bars. There are no tears in my eyes—only the sting of a hot, burning sun.

After school, I ride the bus home in silence. I don't like talking to the other kids who are raucous and rowdy. They're only interested in having fun, while all I want is to get to my bedroom, to be alone. To disappear. Off the bus, I march in my little steps up the tall hill to our house. My sister Kim races ahead, her long, black ponytail flopping in sync with her backpack. Sweat streams down my temples. Mom opens the front door for me while cool, conditioned air rushes across my damp skin. Without a word, I toss my backpack into the hallway and beeline for my bed. Plopping down on my bed, I squeeze my eyes shut, push the boys jeers aside, and try to conjure a very different image.

I find the obscure memory, which floats like mist in a fog: a woman holding my hand. She is saying goodbye, pinning my name to my shirt. In this fabricated memory, I am a toddler, watching my mother walk away, down a long dirty street in the middle of a bleak foreign country.

What is the name of it again? Oh right, Korea—whatever that means. She is leaving me because she loves me, that's what Mom said. I think that is a strange way to love someone.

I squeeze my eyes harder, trying too hard to look around in that memory. Where is the scenery? Are there other people, and do they look like me? Do I feel loved, or simply lost?

I open my eyes, frustrated. Like always, there is no remembering—only guessing, dreaming, and hoping. I don't know anything about Korea except what I've seen Mom watching on the TV show MASH. Only that it's a little country around the world that nobody cares about, where young mothers leave their babies. *Because they are poor. Because they have nothing. Because they love their babies so much they must let them go.* I wonder again, like so many times in my childish mind, why didn't that mother try harder? Why did she only love me enough to leave me, not enough to fight hard enough to keep me?

I wish I could remember just something, anything, about the last day I had with that other woman. But it is gone, and all that I have leftover are the echoes of a boy calling me Chink.

At dinner, Mom asks me how my day at school was.
"Fine."
She asks if anything is bothering me.
"No."

*****

Winter 1987

Today is my birthday! I am ten years old today, and it's already a lucky year for me. I'm lucky because my birthday is on a weekend, so I get my birthday PARTY on my birthday DAY! And I'm lucky because Mom is letting me have my party at home.

Mom never lets people come over to our house EVER. I mean, we have people like Aunt Gail and my neighbor Samantha, but they're just regular. Everyone else is called company and they're not ever allowed, not even if they're just kids from school. Mom doesn't tell me why, but I think it's because Dad's always yelling or sleeping, and plus she doesn't like cleaning the house.

The last time we had company, Mom cleaned the house for two whole days. She put all our normal things in giant boxes and buckets: big rolls of fabric and bags of yarn, and all her baskets full of her "things," and stacks of papers, books, and magazines, and doll collections, and newspapers, and all the trinkets she keeps in jars and different colored bottles, and even more things that we keep all over the floor, tables, couch, and counter. She even moved some of the candles and picture frames, and then she hid everything. I think she probably took them all down to the basement, but since it's already full, I couldn't tell if it was a little bit fuller.

She mopped the floor and even took everything out of the kitchen, but I still can't figure out where she put all that stuff. Then the company came over for a little while, and when they left, everything got put right back where it belonged.

But today she cleaned the house for me, and eight of my friends are coming over. We're going to have cake and watch TV and play games. It's too cold to play outside, and anyways it snowed, so we don't want to get all soggy. But maybe we can have hot chocolate.

It's time for my party to start, but I guess everyone is going to be late. I'm sitting at the kitchen table so I can see as soon as a car turns down the hill into our driveway. I watch and watch and watch. Watching is getting boring, but I'm too excited to be bored because I finally get to have friends in my house! I look at the clock, and it's almost an hour late now, but I think I better stay in my seat because everyone is on their way. Maybe they just got slowed down because of the snow.

It's two hours late now, and I think I should stop watching. I guess something happened and nobody is going to make it after all. I don't know why no one told me. I don't like the sad feeling I have, so I will talk myself out of it. It's okay if no one comes, if I can't really make friends. All princess heroines are lonely, like Cinderella and Sleeping Beauty and Snow White. Anyways, I'd rather be lonely by myself than with a bunch of other kids.

I stand up from the table because it's too late to watch anymore. The cold sun is sinking, and my party that never started is over. I close the door to my room, flop down on my white daybed, and crawl inside the warmth of my book, alone.

Cut

Omma's letter, May 4, 2014

    Then I began to work at the shop in front of my parents' house. One day, one of my neighbors, a man, raped me. I told my aunt about what happened, and she reported it to the police station. But then my aunt criticized me for many days and nights, saying that I made all the trouble. I could not stand the aunt's nagging, so I ran away then and began to work as a maid.

    I worked for three years as a maid here and there. Then when I became nineteen years old, I needed an ID card and missed my family, so I went to my father's house. My dad was so happy to see me. When I ran away, I was sixteen years old, with a height of one hundred forty-three centimeters and weight of less than forty kilograms. I was called by the police, prosecutor, and gynecologist frequently, so I had run away for three years. Anyway, I was happy to meet my father and relatives again. But my neighbors pointed fingers at me and gossiped about me.

*****

Autumn 1989

    I'm in the seventh grade and everything in the world is awful. I never know how I'm supposed to act around other kids, and they can tell how awkward I am. I pretend like I don't care about any of them, that I'm too busy studying or rushing off to something important, or that I have other friends that I'm going to hang out with. I have to turn my back on them before they can turn their backs on me, but usually they don't even notice I'm alive except to make fun of my face or ask me questions I can't answer about being Oriental.

Even worse, we live in this rotten heartland of hoedowns and square dancing. Mom and Dad are determined to keep us connected with our country roots. I can remember classic country music concerts before those songs were classics—where Barbara Mandrell, Charlie Pride, and Conway Twitty would sing and carry us around like dolls. Yeah, we've always been country when country wasn't cool. I'm pretty sure it never will be cool.

Mom and Dad started clogging a few months ago and it means the world to them that Kim and I go to the clogging things with them. For once we all do something together without Dad yelling at Mom and Kim, so how can I complain?

Clogging is so embarrassing though. We practice all the time, which I guess doesn't matter since it's not really cutting into my exciting social life. So practices are okay, but then we have to do performances with the clogging club in public places. For these, we wear matching outfits—all four of us! Mom too! We wear these matching calico dresses with full, ruffled skirts and lacy petticoats. Underneath those, we wear matching bloomers with rows of lace across the butt. The lace gives us a special flair when we twirl.

I could die, but Mom is so happy to have us all doing this together. She thinks I'm so good at clogging, which is a big deal because she never thinks I'm good at anything. Of course she'd never tell me that—she's always bragging how proud she is of me—but I can tell the truth from the way she looks at me and the little stories she tells. For example, she likes to brag that the doctors never thought I'd grow, that I'd be lucky to be as tall as a midget. They told her I'd never have any muscle tone at all because I was only nineteen pounds when I was three years old. Now she looks like she could cry from joy just when she sees me walking across the room.

So, she says she believes I can do anything, but really

I think she's just grateful I'm capable of walking by myself. Her standards of accomplishment are pretty low for me. Clogging—moving my tapped feet fast and hard—is practically a sport for me in her eyes. I'd feel bad letting her down on this.

We're at clogging rehearsal now. I'm so bored I could cry, but she's socializing with the club organizer Clara and the other ladies. They're not even practicing, just talking.

I go to the bathroom and discover something horrible. There's blood in my underwear. I know what this is, since Mom explained it to me when I was eight, although I didn't actually believe something so disgusting could really happen. It's not a question of what, but how? How much will happen? How long will it last? How fast can we get home? I ball up some toilet paper, shove it into the crotch of my little girl underwear, and pull up my jeans. That should last me a little while.

I go back out into the studio where all the ladies are still chatting.

"Mom."

"Just a minute honey."

I wait a minute.

"Mom!"

"What do you need sugar?"

I don't know what to say. I'm too mortified to even tell her, let alone the group of women she's talking to.

"Mom we need to go home."

"Oh we'll be done soon. Just wait."

"No Mom. Really! We need to go home now!" I feel a sticky, hot gush. I think I'm going to either bleed to death or die of humiliation.

"Raina," Mom is getting stern now. "Just wait. Practice isn't over. Go practice or something."

I don't need to practice. I'm really good at clogging. What I need is to sit and never stand up again. What I need is to get home so I can crawl under my bed and melt into a puddle of humiliation. I'm fighting tears as I return to my cold metal folding chair. I feel another gush and squeeze my thighs together.

I wait, and it is an eternity. I'm horrified at my predicament and furious at Mom for not somehow sensing my distress. By this time, maybe my walls have grown too thick for her to see through anymore. I've spent a long time preparing for the rejections that I know this world will hand me—in fact started handing me from the time I was a toddler. I'm ready for the day when Mom loves me too much to keep me, and for every other person who will someday see that I'm not worth holding on to. I've made my heart a stone and my face an empty wall, knowing that I'm best off when left alone.

Finally we leave. I wish Mom could have seen my horror, my anger, my agony at waiting while jeans soaked through with blood. I wish I could say something. Instead, I climb stiffly into Mom's van and sob silently on the dark ride home.

*****

Autumn 1991

Kim has a double sliding-glass closet door. We spend countless hours hunkered amongst piles of teen pop magazines: *Seventeen, Young Miss, Teen,* and *Sassy.* In these pages, I learn how to properly brush my hair, wash my face, apply astringent, select my signature perfume, and dress for a prom that I will never end up going to. What I don't learn is how to apply eye shadow to my hooded eyelids, or how to make my *nigger lips* less puffy, or my *gook eyes* any rounder. No matter how many spiral perms I go for, my hair is always the wrong texture; regardless of how much I tan, my skin is always the wrong shade of brown.

It seems like all the other girls have had boyfriends since we were sixth graders. The beautiful boys and girls pair off and bop around in their bubbles of coolness, of happiness, decked out in their tight-rolled Guess jeans, plastic Liz Claiborne purses, and Eastland loafers.

I'm a pipsqueak, a full year younger than my classmates because I skipped kindergarten. I'm a nerd, trying to pretend every school subject isn't unceasingly boring, pretend that I don't understand even the hardest subjects before the teacher has begun to explain them. But mostly, I'm an outsider even though I've grown up in this town just like everyone else. I'm from a different place, and my face never lets me or anyone else forget it. I hate this face.

I'm too funny-looking to be considered pretty, and it's not until freshman year that a boy expresses an interest in me. It's a confusing situation. I haven't learned to be discriminating, haven't needed to tell a boy no, so I don't know how. I'm flattered by the attention, and sort of embarrassed for feeling flattered. I don't know how to be cool about it, and because I don't know how to say no, I don't. We start dating, which consists mainly of writing silly notes during school and kissing after school. I don't know how to kiss, am I doing it right? Where is the tongue supposed to go? Is it supposed to be slobbery or dry? Is he doing it right?

We sneak into the woods behind school as often as we can. We kiss. He wants to do more, but I don't even know what more is. What leads to what? How do I tell him when to stop, and how do I know when? These are my inadequacies. I've never learned to be a woman. It seems that there are powers that the other girls possess, that they all know about, but it's a club I haven't been invited to. I'm not a normal woman like they are, and so I don't believe in my own feminine powers. I don't know how to control them.

After we make out, I go home feeling dirty and used. Is this what love feels like? I don't believe my heart knows how to feel love anymore, for it has completely grown over with calluses from being overworked, over-chafed. I think I'll never be loved, and I think I'll end up marrying this boy I call boyfriend because he is the only boy who will ever realize I'm alive, who will ever want me.

I descend the stairs to our basement and search. I'm looking for something to help me know if I am feeling love, if I'm feeling anything at all. I find what I'm looking for, a box cutter, and slip it into my pocket. Back up the stairs. Into my room. Close the door. I slide the blade out of its sheath and press it against the dark skin of my forearm.

I cut.

*****

Proof of Love:

If: "We don't know why your birth family couldn't keep you. They must have loved you so much they wanted to give you a better life."

And: "I love you so much."

Then: Love is imaginary

While: Families need children

But: All children, by definition, come from mothers

And: A lost child can't be replaced, but an unborn child should be

Then: Families with interchangeable children are irrational

*****

Summer 1993

My mom is the most enormous character in my world—large, loud, and bold. She stands over five feet, ten inches tall, which is practically a giant compared to me. Mom is always belting out husky baritone choruses of "I can bring home the bacon! Fry it up in a pan! And never ever let you forget that you're a man cause I'm a Wooooahhhh- muuuun! W-O-M-A-N!"

If it's true that most people mellow with age and parenthood, then I can only imagine the personality she was in her youth. As I get older, Mom confides in me about her furious temper and murderous rage—traits that she's not proud of, traits that terrify her. She tells me of boys she used to beat up for disrespecting her family, and I believe her when she says she's willing to both die and kill for me.

Mom tells me how she met the couple that would eventually become Mamaw and Papaw. Dad's parents were steeped in the old ways of Southern, country convention. Their generation had still married first cousins, though they had broken that tradition. They were unwelcoming and judgmental of any woman their darling son dated, for no woman is ever good enough for an only son.

To counter their unfounded prejudices, Mom decided to make her own kind of impression. On the day she was to join them all for dinner, Mom carefully selected the apparel that made her statement from head to toe: Afroed hair, fringed suede vest, skin-tight leather miniskirt, and go-go boots to her knees. Her statement was this: *I'll do as I damn well please, and you'll both respect and love me for it.* It must have worked, because eventually they did.

Because Mom was such a wild thing in her youth, it's hard to imagine what latent part of her would evolve into a pageant mom, but evolve she has. These years later, I can only speculate. Maybe she is motivated by a consuming adoration for her daughters that borders on envy, or maybe she can't resist showing off her real-life China dolls.

We started pageants in elementary school as part of Shepherdsville's annual Olde Tyme Homecoming celebration. Every year Mom dressed us in our most authentic, usually homemade, Southern belle costumes. Here I am, a charming, curly-haired Asian child straight off the plantation in purple ruffled pantaloons with a matching parasol. And there, I'm a hoop-skirted pre-teen, all lace and petticoats, donning dainty fingerless gloves and rows of banana curls. We started the pageants because Mom wanted us to. We keep doing them because, like with the clogging, it makes her happy.

Kim always wins. She holds back her shoulders and holds forth her megawatt smile, and brings home tiaras and trophies taller than me. Mom compares our performances: Kim strides across that stage in a radiant glory, oozing with queenliness, while I stomp across the stage like a farmhand plow girl who has been slapped across the face.

That is, until I finally win one.

Picture the pageant gown first: Mom's meticulous handiwork of red sequins and hand-sewn gold appliqués; long sleeves that are puffed at the shoulders, the body fitted throughout and slit halfway up the right leg. It is a crimson disco ball of a dress.

The hair next: it's short and straight, cropped during one of my rebel phases, so I have worked a small-barreled curling iron all the way around and sprayed it perpendicular from my head to create the illusion of length. The bangs conform to an almost perfectly vertical waterfall cascade.

Now, the stage: rows of high school girls posing in their sparkly gowns and hopeful smiles, feet positioned in strategic pageant t-stances, front knee angled slightly forward to ensure their slimmest silhouettes. To the front of the contestants runs a long catwalk where they will silently demonstrate their Southern charms and grace. To their rear, open pens of competitive livestock—cows, pigs, sheep—are also on display, also vying for blue ribbons, trophies, and validation.

Finally, the announcements: second runner-up, first runner-up, I still don't hear my name. I've lost again. Then, unexpectedly, "The 1993 winner of Miss Bullitt County Fair… is… Raina Chesser!"

Kim is quickly by my side. As the reigning queen she stands at the ready to pass her mantle. I step forward. Kim secures the rhinestone tiara into my hair-sprayed coif, drapes the sash across my shoulder, and fills my arm with roses. Here I am in all my spangled glory, smiling in lightly concealed shame at the measures I'll endure to be recognized as beautiful. The cows moo and sheep bleat their unanimous approval.

*****

In high school, my best friend is Vongduan, the one other Asian kid in school. It's not intentional that we're the only Asian kids, but I don't believe it's a coincidence either.

Vo was born in Laos, the daughter of a policeman and a housewife. The seventies were a violent time in Southeast Asia, and after the abdication of Prince Sisavang Vatthana in 1975, her family became fugitives of the new Pathet Lao regime. Her father hid and planned, and eventually their family made a winding escape through Thailand to Minnesota and then onward to Kentucky.

Our high school allows girls to play on the boys' soccer team to comply with Title IX requirements, and we're the only co-ed team in our region. My parents aren't big sports fans beyond NASCAR, so this first team experience is entirely new for me.

Vo and I enjoy soccer practice, jogging around the field and semi-stalking a player I harbor a secret crush on. But we're terrible at the game, having only started playing on a whim during our junior and senior years because we think the uniforms are cute. Thus, we usually wait patiently on the sideline until our team is losing so badly that there's nothing further to lose by putting us in.

We don't understand the rules all that well either, but we do our best to cheer the team on. Vo and I stand by the bench, both of us at four feet, eleven inches, a full head shorter than most of the male players. Whenever a maroon-clad player dribbles the ball up field, we cheer. When the opponent gains possession, we shriek in dismay.

In a particularly exciting play at the start of the second half during a game early in the season, Vo and I scream wildly as our midfielder inexplicably drives play toward our own defense.

"Wrong way!" we both shout, hoping to save the play. "You're going the *wrong way*!"

After a full minute of our antics—convinced we are helping the team and confused why no one else can see the terrible mistake our team is making—Vo and I abruptly stop screaming. We look at each other at the same moment, simultaneously realizing our embarrassing mistake: *We had switched sides on the field at halftime.* We have been raving like idiotic lunatics.

It takes only moments for us both to erupt into falling-down, gut-busting, breath-catching laughter. Alone, I'd have been mortified. But with Vo, there is no room for humiliation, only hilarity. She is a friend with whom I can easily and unapologetically be myself.

Coach puts us in the last five minutes of the game, along with the other few girls on the team. We never mind the slight—we're simply grateful for the chance to play past the point where we can do harm. After the game, Vo and I head back to her house for a quick dinner.

Vo's mom is in the side yard, squatting on a bench next to a large pot over open flame. She welcomes me with a wave of her long-handled frying strainer and a wide smile that crinkles her eyes. The pot bubbles with hot oil for her legendary egg rolls. Years later, Vo will share the secret family recipe with me: a deep-fried, Laotian rendition of Vietnamese spring rolls that we make by the hundreds. They are bewitching, addictive egg rolls that drive my own friends to accost me for another dose like I am their dealer.

We each grab a handful of the sizzling hot treats and head into the house to prep some salads for dinner. Through the front door, passing Buddhist statues and Laotian wedding portraits en route to the kitchen. I cut the iceberg lettuce and vegetables, while Vo boils and chops eggs. Her father arrives home from work, and I watch them briefly converse in Lao.

Vo's family fascinates me. Somehow, the casual way that she alternates between speaking English to me in one breath and Lao to her parents in the next make her seem more legitimately American than I was. Vo's family is part of a Laotian community in the Louisville area. Through that larger family, she can be a regular American kid while continuing to honor her native country, language, and traditions. The idea of that authenticity without duplicity seems magical to me.

There is quality to Vo's immigrant experience that I envy. Where her identity is a natural adaptation within both her cultures, mine is an adaptation excluded from both of mine. I am ashamed of being Korean and a little guilty about being American. I am a fraud—a first-generation immigrant hiding behind my middle-class white family. I live white privilege by proxy: an Asian child in a white family, an immigrant child in a local household.

On that night, as many others, I linger as long as possible in Vo's home. At home I'm sullen and secluded, and maybe it hurts my parents to have such a distant daughter. It's my way of rejecting them, who have held me so closely yet alienated me so completely with their stifling, unsafe love.

A One-Way Ticket

Omma's letter, May 4, 2014

Anyway, I left my father again and went to Seoul and begin to work to live. Then one day, my married elder cousin asked me to help his wife, as his wife had given birth recently. I was happy to help them. One day, I came back home after meeting with my elder sister. While I was waiting for a bus at the bus stop, a man approached me then dragged me to a nearby mountain, where he raped me. Then he kidnapped me for over a week, and he took me here and there. I could not resist. He locked me in a small room about a month. So I began to live with him. Sometimes he gave me money. Then I became pregnant.

*****

I'm heading to West Point. I'm going to be in the Army.

I imagine that for most kids the decision to attend a service academy is a huge and difficult one. Among other things, they must decide whether they can pass the physical and academic rigors, sacrifice their college years to a military environment, and make the commitment to serve as an officer for five years after graduation. But for a kid with few other prospects, scarce financial resources, and basically no social life, West Point is a no-brainer. The advantages are numerous: escaping Shepherdsville, avoiding college tuition, obtaining a high-quality education, and securing a guaranteed job that will look great on a resume. College, West Point, and the Army are the only way a kid like me gets a one-way ticket out of small-town America. I'll do anything to get out, to finally be somebody.

My sister Kim goes to West Point a year before me,

and in my final weeks of high school, Mom makes mournful jokes.

"I just never dreamed my two little beauty queens would decide to go off to the Army!"

"Most people send their kids off to military school as punishment. Mine volunteer for it. I don't know what that says about how I've done as a parent."

You've never seen someone so proud and so sad.

*****

Summer 1994

I walk across the stage of my high school gymnasium in a maroon cap and gown to receive my diploma. Two quick weeks later, I pack one small gym bag with the few personals that West Point allows, ride twelve hours northeast, and say goodbye to Sheeptown forever. At the age of seventeen years, five months, and twelve days, I step up to the Cadet in the Red Sash and embark on an extraordinary adventure.

The first day at West Point is innocently dubbed Reception Day, which makes it sound a bit like a welcoming party. In reality, the day is anything but hospitable. We shorten the name to R-Day, which is more appropriately similar to D-Day. We new cadets seem to be the enemy.

I am grouped with nine other new cadets—we make up a squad that will eat, sleep, march, and train together for the next 7 weeks of Cadet Basic Training, or Beast Barracks. On R-Day, we move in a line formation that travels through countless processing stations. Barber shops, where young men's heads are shaved and women's hair is cropped above our collars. Uniform issue points, where we are outfitted with a minimum of military clothing that will suffice until our custom-tailored wardrobes are later crafted by a team of specialized Italian clothiers. Medical checkpoints, where we are measured, weighed, inoculated, and deemed fit for duty.

We all wear identical heathered grey t-shirts emblazoned with the USMA crest, black athletic shorts made of stiff polyester, and white gym socks pulled to our knees—the outfit we will come to know as Gym Alpha. We all have a large manila tags pinned to our shorts, to ensure we don't get misplaced or miscategorized. The names written on these tags are the only remnants of our former identities.

Early in the day, we are issued two small books. The first is a tiny hardcover book, embossed with the title *Bugle Notes*. The second is small pamphlet-like book covered in heavy card stock, the *Cadet Leadership Development System* handbook, which is a condensed version of the *Bugle Notes*. These are our bibles for the year. All day we ping—power-walking in straight, purposeful rows between processing stations. Fingers curled at our seams, eyes ahead, no talking. At each station, we wait in endless lines and study the *CLDS* book to memorize the vast random knowledge that will be the foundation of our conversion to cadets, and then Army officers.

There are 78 million gallons in Lusk Reservoir when the water is flowing over the spillway.

The lacteal fluid extracted from the female of the bovine species is highly prolific to the nth degree.

What do Plebes rank? The Superintendent's dog, the Commandant's cat, the waiters in the Mess Hall, the Hell Cats, the Generals in the Air Force, and all the Admirals in the whole damned Navy.

The discipline which makes the soldiers of a free country reliable in battle is not to be gained by harsh or tyrannical treatment.

Always, through the summer of Beast Barracks, we

wear our socks to our knees, ping, sweat, and clutch these tiny books of knowledge.

*****

It's the hottest part of the Hudson Valley summer. The air sags under a heavy sun, full of heat and water that conspire to boil our skin, our minds. Sweat streams from my backside, down my legs, and pools at my calves where camouflage pants are tucked into heavy combat boots. Early August has arrived, and Beast Barracks is almost done. Every one of my squad mates has survived. Together we stand in a platoon formation: poker straight rows of new cadets like myself. Stress, fear, and exhaustion roll off us like a steam. We reek of it.

We've spent the day at the M16 range, learning to fire and maintain our weapons. After arriving back at the barracks, we have 15 minutes to sprint to our rooms, change into clean uniforms, shine our boots, and return for dinner formation. Instead of shining my boots, however, I spend that time sequestered in the barracks bathroom, relieving a stomachache that has plagued me through the day.

Now, in formation before dinner, my squad leader moves through the line, inspecting us one by one. He is two cadets away from me. Now one. Now I am staring straight ahead into his chin. I can count the microscopic black hairs, stubble fighting its way out before it will be shaved back again tomorrow morning. I'm unwilling to meet his eyes in my pathetic state of dirty boots and rumbling stomach. I can feel his eyes moving over my uniform, checking for orderliness, compliance, conformity. He inhales sharply, and I know that he has discovered my mud-and-dust-caked boots.

"Oh. My. God. Chesser. You are so ate up. What's your malfunction?"

I respond with silence.

"Chesser! I'm talking to you! You're a disgrace. What was your mission before dinner?" Spittle flings from his lips onto my hat brim, lands in my short-cropped hair.

I say nothing. There are only four responses that a new cadet is allowed—*Yes sir. No sir. No excuse sir. Sir I do not understand*—and none of them adequately answer his question. Which of those can capture that yes, I understood the mission to clean up but no, I could not accomplish that mission because instead I spent that time desperately crouched on the toilet? How to apologize to my entire squad for the trouble they will all be in now that I have failed our mission to square ourselves away? How to survive the insufferable embarrassment if I mention the truth, that my faulty bowels have deprived my team of big bites, of dessert, of any other good thing that might have come our way today?

In a flash I recall the moment of this evening's demise. Earlier, at the rifle range, sitting in the grass during a fleeting break from drill and training. Daydreaming with my squad mates about all our favorite foods, describing in torturous detail the tantalizing meals of Texas BBQ brisket, NY strip, mountains of crab legs and boiled shrimp. Sharing a tiny box of Cheerios we had smuggled from that morning's breakfast. Watching those Cheerios spill to the ground and, like barbarians, like starving children from hardscrabble streets, scratching handfuls of the cereal up from the ground, swallowing them whole with chunks of dirt and grass. Wondering what I have become, to be so greedy for these few Cheerios. Paying for it now, and dragging my squad down along with me.

I finally settle on the response that seems to best capture the reason for my dirty boots, my turbulent stomach, my greedy hunger, indeed my very existence here at West Point and maybe even in the world. "No excuse sir."

"Pathetic, Chesser. You're a disgrace."

"Yes sir. No Excuse sir."

No excuse. I lose myself in this response. I hide behind it. No excuse. No reason. No justification.

*****

In many ways West Point life is easy for me—there is little challenge in being broken down so I can be built back up. It's just another place, albeit with different expectations, where I only have to conform to be worthy. For me, imitation is as simple as pouring ether from one bottle into another. I become what I am required to be, because I don't yet know what I am.

By the time we finish Beast Barracks and move into the academic year, my brain jangles with randomly memorized quotes from so many generals who came before. Schofield's Definition of Disciple. Worth's Battalion Orders. MacArthur's Message. Scott's Fixed Opinion. Duty, Honor, Country. "The Corps.""The Alma Mater."

Live, serve, and die, we pray, West Point for thee.

Throughout plebe, or freshman, year, we learn so many useful things. How to avoid "breaking sheets" by sleeping on top of our scratchy wool blanket in order to save the time making beds in the early mornings. How to memorize, before 0600, the entire front page of the *New York Times*, the Mess Hall menu, and the countdown of days until every remaining milestone of the year—most importantly the Army-Navy game. How to cut cakes and pies into perfectly even slices based on the number of cadets who wish to eat dessert (odd numbers are the hardest). How to drop a target from 1000 meters. How, if we are to be wrong, then the whole team must be wrong together. There is nothing worse than an individualist.

I have two roommates, Kris and Sharla, both from Ohio. Sharla is twenty-one years old and has a womanly wildness about her. She traipses around our room in her thong underwear joking how her white lingerie makes her feel virginal. Kris is only eighteen years old, and she is laser focused on success. She's tall, blonde, and gorgeous, a varsity volleyball player, and because of those virtues she gets the worst hazing of us all.

The three of us roast together in the pressure cooker of West Point life, and we take refuge in our barracks dorm room. During the days, we don our cadet armor and go to battle—with the upperclassmen, with the Dean, with the 90 percent male cadet population, with the Department of Physical Education, and sometimes with each other. But at lights-out, when we're not pulling all-nighters or collapsing from mental and physical exhaustion, we remove our armor and make ourselves vulnerable to each other.

On one cool spring night like this, late in our plebe year, we lay in our Army bunk beds and fantasize about our futures lives.

"Do you think this is ever gonna get easier?" Kris asks.

"Hell yeah," Sharla answers, "it has to."

I whine, "Y'all think this is really getting us ready for the Army? This can't be what the Army's like."

"Yeah, it completely sucks but there's a reason. Look how much we've already survived. We've made it through so much," Kris adds.

Sharla gets excited about the idea of being an upperclassman. "I know when I get my plebe next year I'm gonna make it hard for him. He's gonna be squared away."

"I don't give a shit about stuff like that," Kris says, "as long as they leave me the hell alone. I've got better things to do than deal with plebes. I'm too exhausted to even think about that. Let's talk about something happy."

We all pause, trying to think of something.

"How do you think we're gonna be in ten years? You guys think you'll still be in the Army?"

"I probably will," I answer. "I haven't really thought of anything else I want to do. It'll be good job security at least."

"I'm not! I'll figure something else out by then! I am NOT a lifer," Sharla is pretty confident about this.

"What about families? Think about it—in ten years me and Rai will be twenty-seven and Sharla, you're gonna be in your thirties! I don't know if I wanna get married."

The thought is astounding to me. "Yeah, I'm not getting married. No way. And I don't ever want to have kids. I can't even imagine."

"Raina don't be stupid, of course you will," Sharla says. "Everyone does."

"No way, not me. I'm not putting a baby in this body and I'm not ever pushing one out."

"Rai! I can just picture you pregnant! Oh my God you'll be so cute. You're like two feet tall," Kris laughs. "Swear to me you'll send me a picture when you're pregnant someday. You have to!"

Sharla agrees. "Yeah, we all have to – the first one who gets pregnant, we'll send a picture. Promise!"

I give in. "Okay, I promise. But only because I know it's gonna be one of you bitches."

*****

Summer 1995

I am young, and feeling beautiful and free for a couple weeks. It is summer break, and I'm home from West Point with nothing to do—no studying, no training, no boots to shine or beds to make—only blissful boredom in my parents' home.

Dad bought a T-top Corvette and she's a stunner. This car has been his life's dream, and every working man should have the chance to fulfill at least one or two working man's desires. She is a deep garnet red, like the imagined blood ties of our family.

"Well go ahead then," Dad says, keys in his hand and a twinkle in his eye. I am confused.

"Eh? Go ahead and what?" I reply.

"Don't you want to drive the Corvette? Come on, let's go for a drive."

I am stunned. Is this a trick? Is he just joking with me? He doesn't trust anyone to breathe near his shiny new toy. He hasn't let anyone even sit in the driver's seat, and now he's handing me the keys?

I slide in behind the black leather driver's seat. I've never seen such luxurious, hand-stitched, top-grain leather. I inhale the newness of this dream car. I'm so low to the ground, I think this is what a hovercraft must feel like.

"Here you go. You can do it. Just keep it below a hundred."

My God. He's really handing me the keys, and I feel a simultaneous rush of terror and exhilaration. I start her up and cruise out of our little Peaceful Valley, on toward the freeway. Once on the open road, I let her rip. My hair is whipping around, the sun has lit my skin from the outside in, and my face is nothing but smiles and teeth. We are flying now, my Dad and me. Suddenly we are every little girl and every father; we are all the goodness and wholeness of family and America and freedom. We are in love with the world but especially this car that has made this moment possible.

We turn off the freeway exit, and Dad tells me to pull into the gas station for a fill-up. We pull in and he hops out to pump the gas. That's when it happens.

I feel the eyes of a stranger crawling on me, invading my moment with my dad. I turn to look and meet the glaring eyes of a middle-aged woman seated in the passenger seat of a car at the opposite pump. At first I think they must be looking past me at something else because I can't understand why she'd direct such pure loathing at me. Then she looks from me to Dad, shakes her head and turns away. Moments later, a man returns and climbs into the driver's seat.

She flings one last malicious look my way, and as they drive away, I see the word mouthed upon her lips: girlfriend.

*****

Spring 2000

West Point is an unexpected place for romance, but there's a handsome young rugby player named Brett who sets his sights on me, and I fall hard. We are an unlikely couple from the beginning, but they say some things are meant to be, and so we are. He's a straightforward, unsentimental man with the practical sensibilities of a Pennsylvania Dutch, Pittsburgh steel town upbringing. In contrast, I'm a complicated mess of repressed emotional hysterics under a façade of stoicism that came from years of holding myself in. Years later, I'll feel a bit sorry for him in retrospect—that young man who didn't yet know what kind of craziness he was asking to marry him.

In May 2000, as fresh college graduates and newly commissioned Army officers, Brett and I marry at Waimea Falls on the north side of Oahu. Two weeks later I board a plane to begin a series of flights toward a faraway nation that was once my first home.

Twenty-somethings exist in a state of nonspecific and unacknowledged terror. At this age, there are a thousand things to be terrified of, the most urgent of which is that we'll completely screw up the beginning of our adult lives just when everything is really starting to matter. At twenty-three, I face not only the frightening chasm between childhood and adulthood, but also a new marriage and my first military assignment as a platoon leader in the abysmal country of my birth.

That's what Korea is to me: an abyss. Months ago, when we were given our selection of first assignment locations, Korea had seemed like a good idea. Why not travel back to the country of my birth wrapped in the protection of my status as American soldier? Why not face the dragons of my past as a newly minted knight in my own spanking new armor? Now that I'm facing the reality of that yearlong duty in Korea, many urgent reasons start to emerge. I realize that, no matter how big and grown I think I am, I'm still a frightened child deep inside. With age has come the experience of how to hide that frightened child, or stuff her head under a pillow so she'll shut up, but ultimately she's still there, just waiting for that opportunity to bring me to my knees.

And does she ever. A few months before my one-way flight to the Land of the Morning Calm, I am paralyzed with terror. While Raina, nearly grown and reasonably accomplished, was sure that a tour in Korea could be no worse than the trials of West Point and the horrors of small town high school, Soojung has objections. She remembers Korea as a land of despair and rejection, a place where love means leaving. Returning only means she'll have to again face all those losses she's spent so many years outrunning.

*****

There is no simple way to travel from Shepherdsville to Seoul. First, you have to drive the hour commute from

Shepherdsville to Standiford Field in Louisville. From there, Delta Air Lines will take you to Dallas-Fort Worth and then onward to Los Angeles International Airport. Then it's a short hop up to San Francisco, over to Narita, Japan, and finally to Gimpo International. Time traveling from the present to a future that lies in the past is never a simple matter.

At LAX, I sit with my military orders and holographic green US Army ID card in hand, my olive drab duffel bag at my feet. I focus all my energy on keeping a blank mind, which is the only way I can manage the persistent dread in the small of my belly. I stare at that duffel bag with force.

"Heading to Korea?" The man seated next to me startles me with his friendliness.

"Um, yes sir."

"Just got married, eh?"

How could he know that?

"Um, yes sir," I'm not feeling too articulate.

"I could tell by your ring. Could spot it a mile away. Brand new, not a mark on it yet."

"Yes sir. Married two weeks ago in Hawaii. The last time I was in this airport was on my way to get married."

"Well, it won't be easy but you'll be fine. I was stationed in Korea once and had a great time. It's a beautiful country. Such wonderful people. Lots of great shopping."

I don't care about the shopping, but I'm relieved to hear something positive about the country that I dread.

I've been on plenty of planes before. The first was the one that carried me away from Korea and made me an American adopted daughter. Since then, mostly thanks to the Army, I've flown to Europe, South America, the Caribbean, Southern California, the Middle East, and Hawaii. By now I am sure of two things: the place I love best is the inside of a book, and the places I hate most are airports. In airports, I'm either being left behind or leaving something else behind. Either way, airports are places of losing, and airplanes are vehicles of loss.

As my flight approaches the Korean peninsula, the flight crew reminds us to return our seats to their upright and locked positions, turn off portable electronics, and stow our loose items in preparation for landing. Although my arrival at Gimpo International is in the early afternoon and I have an intellectual understanding of time zones and Earth's rotation, I'm still stunned to realize that outside my porthole the sun is actually shining. This small fact—that the sun is not only bright but even has the audacity to be cheerful about it—is my first indication that, despite twenty years of nightmares, Korea might not be a black hole on Earth.

I spend a year stationed as a platoon leader at Camp Laguardia in Uijongbu, a small town halfway between Seoul and the DMZ. In a swift progression through dread, trepidation, cautious enjoyment, and finally sheer joy, I climb out of my terror and into the bright sunshine. This is not the same Korea I had left as a child.

In the years between my birth and my return—1977 through 2000—Korea underwent an unprecedented transformation from second-world country to technological giant. Everywhere you go in Korea, you hear the words *Palli! Palli!* or *Hurry! Hurry!* The older generation pride themselves on this phrase and its symbolism. They attribute Korea's remarkable post-war recovery and then economic ascension to that industrious sense of urgency. This simple word embodies the determination of a broken but proud nation to throw off its history and create a new fortune.

*****

"Palli! Palli!"the young man next to me urges the taxi

driver to speed faster. My vision is vague and blurry; time and light keep zooming in and out. I am wedged between two American men in the back of a Korean taxicab. We are army lieutenants, none of us a breath over twenty-five and having the time of our lives in a country that can't get enough of our drunken Yankee dollars. It must be sometime after 2 a.m. because the Korail train has stopped running for the night. We make our way by cab northward to Dongducheon, where these two lieutenants are stationed at Camp Casey.

We've spent God knows how long up to no good, stumbling up and down Hooker Hill, Itaewon's expat playground. I'm stoned out of my mind on liquor and cigarettes. As always, the poison I pick is a cataclysmic cocktail of soju and Tang served in a sawed-off half-gallon plastic jug. Soju is a sneaky bitch. She fills your mouth and mind with her seductive sweetness, and at the moment when you are at your highest and happiest, she cuts you off at the knees. She is the absinthe of East Asia.

Because of soju, I can't think and I can barely see. The cab and the young men are swirling around me in a slow-motion cartoon carnival. They say we need to get to Toko-Ri before all the best places close. I haven't been to Toko-Ri, but like usual I'm game for anything. The rules of this boys' club are the same everywhere: go along to get along. Be one of the guys, be a chameleon, don't make waves, keep everyone happy. Make them believe you're a cool girl. Hold on tight! It's a wild ride from one hellhole of American depravity to another!

We are here now, in the seediest of clubs. The crowd is sparse and scattered, small drunken groups are huddled in corners and shadows. I notice that the men I arrived with are gone. The dim orange-red light and half-dressed girls act as a bucket of cold water over my burning conscience, and suddenly I'm feeling stone sober. I sit and sway on a couch and wonder where everyone went. I see one now, dancing with one of the "drinky girls" as we American soldiers call them. Where is the other? My head is heavy and I want to lie down, but the couch is an oddly stained shade of green vinyl, and I'll never be so drunk or tired as to place my face against whatever else has lain there.

I want to leave. I'm done for the night, and every cell and particle of my being is rebelling against this place. I make a plan to use the ladies' room then catch a cab away from here—to anywhere that is safe.

It's in the bathroom where I see her, and I understand. She's a young woman about my age, barely older than a girl. I guess she might be Thai or Filipina. I've heard the rumors that women are lured into Korea with promises of legitimate jobs and then indentured to work at the clubs that we Americans visit. I haven't thought much of it—I have my own things to worry about, like running my platoon, keeping in touch with my long-distance newlywed husband, and numbing myself to so much love and hate for this country. But I see her right in front of me, and I am forced to look into her eyes.

She is squatting above a drain grate in the floor, her skirt pulled up around her hips with no underwear beneath. She uses one hand to hold a cut hose, the other to wash herself in the place that her underwear should be. I see her now, as I've never seen anyone before. I see deadness in her eyes, hopelessness and need that threaten everything I think I know of the world and myself. I see an alternate universe where we are the same person: I am her and she is me and we are both every girl and woman in the world. I can see through her eyes, and through them I see myself staring back in drunken horror—just an ignorant, indulgent child.

We only share a moment, but in those seconds rest the whole of my life. We are only feet apart, yet in that space there are universes between us. I see her now, I understand, and I will always bear the shame.

*****

In many ways, the life of an American soldier in South Korea is monotonous. I am assigned to a Combat Engineer battalion in the Second Infantry Division. In units like mine, almost everyone is a geographical bachelor living in the barracks on post. The officer and NCO quarters, where I live, could generously be described as studio apartments. More accurately, they are tiny cinder block rooms with basic, military issue furnishings: a twin bed, a solid wood dresser, a beige laminate dinette, two dining chairs, a couch, and a TV stand (where instead of a television, I store stacks of my beloved books). You can clear the entire span of the room in eight long strides.

I am a platoon leader of seventy-five soldiers in what the Army called an Assault Float Bridge company. Five days a week, we perform early morning physical training and then move on to mission training or motorpool maintenance on our fleet of Mark V boats, floating bridge sections, and HEMTT military trucks. Every couple of months we load up all our gear—GP medium tents, portable kitchen units, boats, and bridges—to play in the Imjin River for weeks at a time. These field exercises are immersive opportunities to hone our skills and enjoy the life of soldiers in training. We go out regardless of extreme weather conditions—monsoons and sweltering humidity are no constraints for a forward-deployed army ready for war. When it's too cold to run boats through the river, we conduct ice-cutting operations in temperatures as low as -30F. The days are sometimes wearisome but always fulfilling.

Between the weeks of training, the weekends are glorious. My closest friend here is a fellow lieutenant and West Point grad, Melanie. Mel, as we call her, approaches her world as if every day is an escapade. She was born and raised in Hawaii and that spirit of aloha never got drilled out of her. Even when Mel stands at the head of her platoon issuing military orders, she maintains that devilish twinkle in her eye, as though just on the verge of cracking up and ordering them all into a massive military bear hug.

With the help of Mel's adventurous spirit, it is a whirlwind year. Every weekend is a quest. We explore Gyeongbokgung Palace and kneel in mountainside Buddhist temples, and both are like ancient places I have known in my dreams, that I somehow know with my soul. We follow winding hiking trails up the Seoraksan and Soyosan mountains, where I clutch at the rocky trails and just when I think I'll plunge to my death on the jagged rocks below, an ancient ajumma trots by in high heels. We trek the long road up to Namsan Tower, where we transition from squatty potties at the bottom to magnificent views of Seoul at the top.

We ride white water rapids in yellow inflated rafts with locals who speak barely more English than we do Korean. We barter at the markets of Namdaemun and Dongdaemun where I learned that even a hundred-pound American like me is too fleshy to squeeze into jeans cut for the fashionably emaciated. We got lost in the meat and fish markets of Uijongbu where every step and turn through the soggy streets brings an onslaught of exotic and strange new slabs of pungent mystery flesh.

But what we do best is eat. Oh, the glorious meals! Mel and I spend our year in one of three conditions: planning our next meal, gorging ourselves on the present meal, or savoring the memory of our most recent or favorite meal.

Korean cuisine is unabashedly bold. It arrogantly declares that, no matter what wars or occupations, whether the country itself is cut in half and its people beaten and scattered, the food will nourish and rebuild and reclaim its people. The food is an evangelism of the palate, and Mel and I are giddy converts.

We hike miles in ice and snow to sit on the hot *ondol* floors of our favorite restaurants, around low *bapsang* tables with built-in grills. We eagerly wait for our cauldrons of *dakbokkeumbap*—spicy chicken and potatoes—to bubble into a stewed perfection. We ride the train for an hour south just to have a taste of the all-you-can-eat *bulgogi* and *samgyeopsal* buffets, where we learn to fold immaculate lettuce-wrapped parcels to deliver grilled meats, hot pepper paste, and steaming rice to our eager mouths. We luxuriate in tiny bowl after bowl of various *banchan*, our tables laid heavy with cucumber, *oi sobagi*; cold sprout, *gongnamul*; spinach, *sigeumchi namul*; daikon radish, *kkakdugi*; and spicy, garlicky, pungent, ubiquitous cabbage, *kimchi*. The flavors of Korea make me whole.

Although my mind and body had arrived when I cleared customs at Gimpo, it takes a whole year, bite by bite, for my soul and spirit to finally begin their wayward path home. Over heaping bowls of *bibimbap*, *soondubu*, *japchae*, and *naengmyeon*, I find that both my two halves—all-American Raina and lost Korean Soojung—began to acquaint themselves to one another. This is the power of a great meal, to reconcile even the bitterest of enemies.

*****

Every night in Korea, I hold a silent, solitary ritual in my barracks room. I drink a beer, I smoke a cigarette. I process the world from which I came, I integrate the parts of myself. I heal.

What I do not do is wonder about my Korean family. I don't ask my American family to send information about the orphanage where I had lived as a young child. I don't seek out my "finding place" where I was supposedly discovered by the police; I don't even bother to learn its name. In the whole twelve months of living in my birth country, I take no steps closer to learning about my history, but in some ways, at least, I stop turning away from   it.

Part 2
Reparation

"There is no comfort anywhere for anyone who dreads to go home."

~ Laura Ingalls Wilder

A Biological Narrative

Omma's letter, May 4, 2014

Then one day, my cousin found me on a small street by chance. Subsequently, my sister found me at the kidnapper's house and took me to the hospital for an abortion. Then I stayed with my sister for few days. After my sister went to work, I went to my kidnapper's house. My sister came to the kidnapper's house and pulled my hair and beat me. Neighbors tried to stop my sister from beating me, but she shouted at them, "Would you keep calm if your younger sister lived with this old SOB?" When my sister tried to take me back to her home, I told her that I preferred to live with the kidnapper.

A few years later, I became pregnant again and went to my sister's house. This time my sister accepted me as I was, but I could not remember many things since I was kidnapped. I could only remember my sister's beating. Anyway, at 1:00 p.m., on February 15, 1977, I gave birth. It was a cold day, and my baby was born at a maternity home in Myeonmok-dong.

*****

Brett and I celebrate our one-year marriage anniversary in the same week that I return from my army assignment in Korea, and we move into his little apartment at Fort Hood, Texas. Although we've already been married a year, we barely know each other. Thus, we get busy getting to know each other right away—so busy, in fact, that we find ourselves pregnant within a month.

I've never wanted to be a parent. In the letters we sent back and forth across the Pacific Ocean, we had debated about when to start having children. My argument was simple and consistent: we shouldn't.

For me, the notions of family have always been complicated. The definition of the word evades me like fog. Most adults I know cannot pull apart the concepts of parental love and biological kinship as viewed from the child's perspective. Many have not experienced love and biology as mutually exclusive concepts and are therefore deeply ingrained to combine them in the same way we insist that oranges must be the color orange. Those who were raised by biological parents don't always realize that "parent" carries multiple definitions—the roles and actions of a person who nurtures, loves, and parents a child versus the spiritual and almost instinctive way that the parent is biologically linked to the child. Even if one does understand this duality at an academic level, the deeply personal and emotional implications cannot be understood until the two concepts are cleaved apart.

Because my biological narrative was broken, I came to understand at a fundamental level that I am not unique—I was any child from any orphanage, and my family didn't need *me*, they just needed a parentless child. I was a replacement child, and therefore replaceable.

For all these reasons, I can't make sense of why people should care about each other just because they are related by blood. To a person who doesn't have blood relatives, blood is meaningless. Mothers leave their daughters and strangers claim other people's children. In my world, people change their minds about family, and therefore nothing is safe or lasting. In my world, I am just as related to everyone as I am to no one. Within that framework, it just doesn't make sense to have children of my own. Not only that, but it feels a little irresponsible because I'm not qualified to teach someone else how to be family.

The day I first suspect I'm pregnant, I immediately purchase a two-pack home pregnancy test. When both of those prove positive, I return to the store and purchase more. It takes five little white test sticks with ten thin pink lines to convince my brain what my body already knows: I am hosting an alien invader.

I slip into a numb terror, ashamed of my own stupidity in allowing this to happen. Haven't I argued for months that I don't want to have kids? And yet here I am just one month into cohabitation, and in the Texas heat I am literally barefoot and pregnant. I despair at the prospect of becoming a mother, and then I anguish at being the type of person who would feel that way. I take my shame and pile it up on the floor in the middle of our apartment and wallow around in it. I pull it up around my neck and head like a blanket and hide inside it like a thief.

Then I make a decision. I decide that my opinion on the topic doesn't matter, for when have I ever gotten a vote? Family—whatever that means—is not something you choose, it is something that is chosen for you. So I will do what I have always done and be the good daughter, good wife, good soldier, and now good mother.

I crawl from my nest of shame and set my head on straight. I wipe away tears and fears, fold them into a tissue and flush it down the toilet. Then I set about the business of making the news a joyous surprise for Brett.

*****

Three hours after the World Trade Center falls, I am lying on a table in the Darnell Army Hospital with an ultrasound wand smearing clear, warm goop against my still-flat belly. The room is dark and small, the ultrasound monitor throwing a cool green glow against the walls. Brett and I watch the technician closely. She smooshes the goop this way and that, pausing occasionally to clack on a computer keyboard or print-screen certain angles of the grainy black and white image on the monitor. I strain to see, but I can't decipher any comprehensible form in the images that are supposed to be the alien in my belly.

Finally, the ultrasound tech stops and faces us. Her broad grin reaches all the way to the crinkles of her eyes. She must have done this thousands of times, and yet she still takes joy in showing nervous, new parents the first images of their unborn children. She moves the mouse arrow on the monitor and pointes at various white speckled blobs on the screen.

"There we are! Here is the profile, and here is the butt and the legs."

She draws a circle around what looks like three short lines on the screen.

"And that tells us… Are you sure you want to know?"

"YES!" Brett and I urge. We don't like surprises.

"Well those lines tell us you have a girl. Congratulations!"

A girl. I hold that thought for a moment; I let it float clear and lonesome in my mind before all the other thoughts rush in after. A daughter, like me.

The months go by and my belly grows. I look as though a flesh-colored, twenty-pound watermelon is hung on my four-foot, eleven-inch frame. When the child inside me goes into her calisthenics, that watermelon becomes a tsunami. I understand how Sigourney Weaver must have felt in *Alien* just before the monster sprang from her stomach.

Near the end of my pregnancy, I recall the promise I made to my two roommates a lifetime ago at West Point. I am the first of our plebe trio to become pregnant. By now I have completely lost touch with Sharla and hadn't had contact with Kris in years, but I send an awkward pregnancy photo to their last email addresses I have on file.

*****

Spring 2002

Our daughter is born. We name her Malia June, a name that came to me in a dream, a name that honors Brett's grandmother June who passed away during my pregnancy.

Malia comes into the world swollen, pink, and angry as hell. We seem to be equally shocked to meet each other, and to realize there really was a human being on the other end of that umbilical cord.

I don't do all those things that new moms are supposed to do, like counting her perfect little fingers and toes or fall breathlessly in love. I once read in a book that new moms enjoy watching their children sleep, but I find the effort is boring and makes me nod off too.

I don't even think to change her diaper until the last day of our hospital stay, but thankfully the nurses have been taking care of those details. When the hospital staff lets me strap her into a carrier seat contraption and tells me to go home, I can't believe they are serious. Surely they don't trust this tiny human to me.

I spend those first days and months of motherhood in a tired state of ambivalence. I sleepwalk through the maternal motions for her benefit, not mine: breastfeeding, skin-on-skin-bonding, cleaning and sucking snot with the bulb of torture— I execute these duties with nurse-like efficiency. Mostly, though, I feel sad about my sudden conversion to legitimate, responsible adult. If God gave me the option to go back to my pre-baby life, I'd seriously consider it for a minute. I'm not proud of this, but I'm not ashamed of it either. These are the emotions of new motherhood.

All the while, I study Malia to find traces of myself. I search her like a map, looking for clues to validate me: the shape of her hands and feet, the texture of her skin, already so much like mine. She is a tiny, miraculous extension of myself—a resumption of my disrupted biological narrative.

"Hello there, baby," I eye her suspiciously.

"Gah-ahhh!" Malia gurgles with her strange, toothless grin. She looks to me like a miniature, feminine old man, and this strikes me as deliriously funny.

"Well, here we are. I'm your mom. Sorry about that."

"Ooooohhhhhgggggghhh," she replies, shoving three toes into her gummy mouth.

"You know, you're not that bad really. I thought you'd be cuter, but I'm sure you'll outgrow this weird phase. Maybe when your comb-over grows out, you'll look a little more normal. By then maybe I'll be more normal too. I have to get used to this mom thing. I'm not like Grandma. She knew what she was doing. I know you've only been alive for a little while, but I'm already starting to forget what it was like without you. Guess that means something right?

"I'm your family, kiddo. You're my family. I've never had family before, not this kind I mean. I have Grandma, Grandaddy, and Aunt Kim, but I never had family that was related to me. I've always just been me, like an island. Now you're here. Welcome to my island, baby. Would you like a mai tai?"

Malia passes gas and smiles in ignorant gratitude.

Two years later Ty is born, and two years after that our baby Cade is born. In that way I begin a slow transfiguration from myth to reality. These children dismantle the fortress of me, one stony wall at a time. So long ago, my mom told the story of how her daughters had repaired her broken heart, and now I understand this strange magic.

Like a velveteen rabbit, I become real through the power of children's love.

Summer, 2006

I miss the Army. It's been about a year since I last wore the battle dress uniform, and I miss the familiar feel of the starched creases. I miss the anonymity of the camouflage uniform along with the simplicity of having name, rank, and unit sewn onto my shirt.

Now I have shed the military skin that I wore for twelve years and have donned another: army to civilian, BDU to corporate suit, combat boots to dress heels, dog tags to business cards. I'm a master of disguise, a soldier hiding inside a civilian woman's body, an American hiding in a Korean's body. Or has it been the other way around?

We've relocated the family from Texas to Tennessee as we embark on our new civilian life. I'm at a business conference for financial planners, grabbing at the first career opportunity before me. I don't know it yet, but this is just one in a stream of career restarts before I'll finally get it right six years later.

There seem to be hundreds of us sitting in these neat rows of chairs, all pointed forward to follow the speakers at the head of the room. The brocade patterned carpet screams at my feet, the florescent light tears at my eyes, and the thinly padded conference chair stabs at my aching back. Mostly though, this suit and this life feel all wrong.

Finally, after a parade of presentations about securities, options and derivatives, we break. I step outside the hotel conference room to a large lobby-like area where snacks and drinks sweat in ice buckets. I secure a water bottle and plate of fruit, and then move off to the side of the room, unsure of how to engage with these strangers around me. The civilian business world might as well be a foreign country, and I don't speak the language.

A tall man with salt-and-pepper hair makes his way toward me. As he approaches, I try to stand tall and confident in my new Ann Taylor suit. I'm about to engage with a native.

"Well hi there!" He drawls in his slow, Southern accent. "Thought you looked lonely; thought I'd keep ya some company."

I smile in response. I am a nervous smiler. "Hi, I'm Raina. Nice to meet you."

We shake hands. I dread the upcoming chat; small talk is torturous for me.

"Well, sugar, I just couldn't help but come over and talk to ya. Thought you might be interested in somethin'."

"Uh thanks? Sure?" I have a feeling I might not be that interested.

"Well I jus thought ya'd like to know, I got myself an Oriental wife just like you."

My smile freezes on my lips.

"Yeah I been married a few times an' I got tired of that. Thought, I need myself a good oriental woman. So looked on the Internet an' I found one on a website. Went over to China a few years ago to meet 'er, brought 'er back an' got married. Just as happy as can be now."

I'm still frozen to my spot next to the wall that refuses to swallow me up, no matter how desperately I wish for it to.

"Oriental women, now y'all really know how to keep a man happy. Got the right values 'n all. Ya married?"

I edge around the corner wall, fuming inside. I don't answer his question.

My mind is screaming now, I'm your colleague! I graduated from West Point. I was an officer! I'm more American than you are, you disgusting, filthy, racist old man! But I say nothing. I've never been able to say anything in moments like this. All my best comebacks hit me hours after the moment has escaped.

I am past him now, scurrying away as fast as these clumsy heeled shoes allow. How I wish they were boots, and I was back in a world that saw me only for the value of my education and leadership, not the shape of my eyes or the color of my skin.

*****

When you become a parent, the universe reveals to you a few of its universal truths. The first is that no one has a clue what they're doing. I grew up believing that adults—in particular, parents—had everything figured out. So in the hospital I expected some magic fairy dust of knowledge to snow around my head and shoulders, bestowing me with maternal instincts and wisdom. I expected to be transformed from the self-centered adult-child that I was. In reality, I just became a self-centered adult-child with a baby. There is no fairy dust of knowledge; we all have to learn for ourselves.

Once I realize this about parents, I start seeing glimmers of that same truth in other areas of my life. My ranking army officers, my soldiers, the elderly checkout guy, even my own mom (whom I had once believed was both omniscient and omnipotent)—like me, they were just figuring it out as they went. Turns out, we're all stumbling along and doing the best we can. That little bit of wisdom goes a long way in helping me relate to others in a meaningful way and be kind to myself.

That first truth leads you to the second truth, which is that everyone comes into this world covered in baby slime and shitting themselves. That is to say, although our words, actions, or accomplishments eventually diverge down the road, we all start in basically the same place. No one is intrinsically more valuable than anyone else, and with the exception of perhaps a few truly evil people, we're all fundamentally good. It helps me to remember that, especially about my kids, especially when they're trying to kill each other, burn down the house, and ride our dogs like small ponies. It also helps when I'm dealing with an especially challenging person to imagine them as they started life: with their ankles up in the air, getting their ass wiped clean. Everyone was once someone's baby.

I have a period of about seven years—the baby-making and newborn years—in which my memory is like a puddle of mud. Anne Lamott once wrote that babies are born clutching a fifth of your brain in their tiny hands, so by my calculations I lose about fifty percent of my mind between 2002 and 2006.

I won't bore you with stories of how cute, funny, or smart my kids are because the third universal truth is that nobody on Earth is actually interested in other people's kid stories. We all listen patiently and feign delight so that we can have a turn, like debits and credits in the Bank of Parental Bragging. There's nothing wrong with this—it's an efficient and beneficial system. But since there's no way for you to have your turn spinning some boring kid stories, I'll spare you mine.

What everyone really wants to do, but not everyone gains the courage for, is to be real. By now, I've participated in enough baby showers, book club meetings, and moms' nights out to recognize the pattern.

Mom #1: "Sarah is such an amazing kid. You won't believe what she said the other day and blah blah blah blah blah blah. There's just no other kid in the universe like her!"

Other Moms: "Mmmm hmmm. Oh how funny. My goodness! Mmmm hmmm."

Mom #2: "Well that reminds me of the time that Jared blah blah blah blah blah blah blah blah blah, and he just kills me when he does that!"

Other Moms: "Mmmm hmmm. Oh how funny. My

goodness! Mmmm hmmm."

Rotate moms and repeat.

Finally, arriving late with two bottles of vodka and a mysterious rust-colored stain across the front of her pants, a truth-teller arrives: "HO-LEEE SHIT ladies! Sorry I'm late. Those bastards just wouldn't stop fighting and I tried to ignore them, but then I noticed that Ella got Claudia on the ground and wouldn't stop kicking her in the stomach. So I had to break them up before she broke her sister's ribs, and I finally got fed up and locked them in the backyard and I told them, 'No one's allowed back inside until one of you kills the other one! Winner can come back in!' Well that shut them up, and they just stood there staring at me with bewildered looks on their faces; turns out they don't really want to kill each other after all. Here everybody, cheers! Mommy needs a drink!"

At that point the Stepford-wife masks come off and you see the life sort of snap back into everyone. Then it really gets going, everyone spilling their guts and telling their truths and showing their actual faces, which are not delightfully perfect, but are beautifully real and covered in hard-earned scars and occasionally a smear of baby milk vomit or mustard-yellow poop. That's when we start understanding and healing one another, and we begin navigating our way together through this labyrinth of parenthood and life.

I don't mean to say that parenthood is bad and children are awful. But we should recognize the everyday miracle that, no matter how much our kids make us crazy, or how sticky they leave the refrigerator door and toilet seat, or even when all of them have the stomach flu at the same time, we love these children of ours. They keep our hearts beating, and that is something about the meaning of family.

*****

Summer 2006

When Brett and I get out of the Army, we try on many different jobs and cities. We drag Malia and Ty from Fort Hood, Texas, to Murfreesboro, Tennessee, and soon after that we again drag them down to St. Augustine, Florida, where we start building a life. I've been a mother for five years, now with three children, and I'm finally giving myself permission to remove my own Stepford-wife mask. There is no such thing as perfection.

It's a swampy Florida morning and I have just dropped the kids at daycare on my way to work when my phone rings. On the other end of the line is Kris, my old college roommate who is now one of my best friends. We kept in touch off and on after reconnecting over my dreadful pregnancy photo, and through that connection we discover we have so much more in common as adults than we did as teenagers. Kris was adopted too (domestically) and when she enters her own pregnancy, our friendship strengthens over wine and discussions on the meaning of family, the significance of parenthood, and how we can manage to have it all.

Kris and I look like actors in a romantic comedy—she is the striking lead actress, and I'm the dorky sidekick. Where Kris is tall and graceful, I'm short and awkward. Where she is all Scandinavian blondes and brilliant blues, I'm a muddled palette of browns. Kris glows like the sun while I thrive in shadows; she is center and I am margin. We are so unalike that we eventually come full circle to sameness.

I see her name on my phone and answer, "Hey Kris!"

"Hey Rai. You have a few minutes? I need to talk."

"Yeah sure, I'm on my way to work. How's it going? Hanging in there?"

"Actually, Rai, I'm not doing so great. I need to get

your thoughts on something."

Kris is in the weeds of those first few months of new motherhood, so I suspect I know what's on her mind. "What's up?"

"I just need you to tell me I'm not crazy. I know I'm supposed to be happy now, but I'm so miserable. I mean, I'm not depressed or anything, just unbelievably unhappy. I can't talk to Joe about it. He's so over-the-moon happy and everything's so good and easy for him because he doesn't *do* any of the work. I'm pissed at him all the time, and he's just stupid with happiness. I can't stand him right now. I feel so alone."

I take a breath. Where to start?

"First of all Kris, you're absolutely not crazy, and Joe's really not horrible either. I know exactly what you're going through, and I bet plenty of other moms do too. It's just that none of us talk about it. Remember how no one bothered to explain about episiotomies until it was too late? Same thing.

"Brett was the exact same way. When Malia was newborn his idea of taking care of her was to play PlayStation with her in his lap. I don't think he meant to be an ass about it, but that's how it felt. I sort of hated Brett those first couple years. That was probably the worst time of our marriage, and we fought all the time."

For the first time, I admit these secret truths. I've spent all these years keeping our new-parent struggles private–the fighting, resentment, and loneliness. Where I'd once been an equal partner in our marriage, as a new parent I felt devalued. I had resented Brett's ability to be selfish when I had wanted selfishness for myself, and I understand the resentment Kris is building against Joe.

"How do you deal with that? It's not fair. It's not like I *want* to do the baby work more than he does. You guys seem okay now. What changed?" Kris asks.

"Well you can't change the fact that you have a baby,

and you can't change Joe right now. Your baby's in the 'loaf of bread' phase; all she does is lie there and eat and poop. I promise it gets better when she's older and starts running around and being fun, because that's when Joe will get more involved. You can work on him over time, but you're just making yourself miserable by thinking it's going to be different right now.

"You have a choice. You accept it and move forward, or you make the same mistakes as me and fight it and be completely miserable. Either way, it's gonna go the way it's gonna go."

Kris is silent a few moments. These are the days before mom snark will become mainstream—before books like *Sippy Cups Are Not for Chardonnay* and blogs like *Rants From Mommyland*, when moms are still pretending everything is great and we can do it all. I can sense something shifting in her from hearing these truths, as I feel my own shift from speaking them for the first time.

She goes on, "It's just hard when everyone only wants to tell me how lucky I am. Like the only option is to be completely happy. Is there some rule that we're supposed to be instantly overjoyed and selfless the second we give birth? Cause, honestly Rai, I feel more alone than I've ever felt in my whole life."

"Oh Kris, you're not alone at all. The problem is that we don't tell each other how lonely we are, how hard and how much work it is. I think as a culture we screw each other by pretending everything's perfect. I was so miserable when Malia was born. I spent a lot of time wishing I could undo it, and then I felt like a horrible human being for feeling that way. But I suspect a lot of other people feel this way because we can't be that abnormal. No one says it, but it has to be true.

"Maybe if we talk about it more, we can help make it more normal. Because we're not terrible people, we don't hate our kids. We're just sacrificing and growing up faster than anyone is really capable of. It doesn't mean you can't love your baby, I just think it takes time to learn it."

I remain in my car long after arriving at the office parking lot, talking through these many difficult, universal feelings of new motherhood with my dearest friend. No one has asked me to tell my truth before, and once I start I can't seem to stop. On this day, Kris and I both develop a new addiction: telling our truths, and really hearing the truths of others.

*****

Spring 2009

Running errands with the kids. It's a hot, exhausting day, and the humidity is making us all melt. The kids vote on where we will eat lunch—two votes for Tropical Smoothie. Cade is only two years old, so we throw out his vote for McDonalds.

We pull into a strip mall, and the kids pile out like clowns from a circus car: Malia, 7; Ty, 5; Cade, 2. So much energy, expectation, and hope in these little people of mine. At the sidewalk outside of Tropical Smoothie there is a small gathering of teen and pre-teen boys. I'm fussing with Cade's shoes and take little notice of them.

One of the boys calls in our general direction, "Ching chong hing hong mei gei mooooo." The other boys laugh.

Just like that, in an instant, I'm nine years old again. I'm on the playground, and the other kids are asking how I can see out of my slit eyes, how I can breathe out of my flat nose, and if I eat dog. They are pulling back the corners of their eyes and smashing down their noses; they are singing ching chong. I hear words like gook and chink and jap, jokes like "Wax on, wax off" and "Orphan Annie."

Then I come back to myself. Those days are over. I've served my country, earned my citizenship, and my family is the epitome of Americana. I give no one the power to demoralize me, let alone some pubescent, asshole punk kids. I swallow my humiliation and replace it with outrage; I have been treated like a foreigner for too long, and I will not pass that legacy on to my children. I have to set an example for them, and it will be an example of strength and righteousness.

I stop walking. I turn back toward those boys with all my children in tow. I stand before those boys and young men, and I teach them a lesson in manners, respect, and citizenship.

*****

Winter 2008

Two weeks before Christmas, I book a last-minute flight from Jacksonville, Florida, to Louisville, Kentucky. Mom greets me at the gate with a hug, and we walk silently to her midnight blue Scion, which bears her familiar aroma of lingering cigarette smoke.

She bought this car over four years ago on an emergency trip to Texas, where we were stationed at the time. I had been induced five weeks before my due date, and Brett couldn't make it home from Iraq in time for the birth of our second child. As soon as I had called them with the news, Mom and Dad jumped into their van and drove south for thirteen hours through the late August heat. They made it just in time to witness my first son's birth, and also to deliver me Chili's Steak Fajitas and Outback Aussie Cheese Fries. Fifteen hours of induced labor made for a hungry momma.

Mom and Dad had rushed into Texas driving the van, and on a whim they had added the Scion to their car collection. I always associate that car with the vitality of my son's birth and the faithfulness of my parents.

But this time we ride her Scion in Louisville's frozen December, racing toward my grandmother's death. *Everything points back in the same direction,* I think. *Birth and death, joy and grief. Always speeding away from one and toward the other.*

"How are you?" I glance over. In addition to the exhaustion and grief etched into her face, Mom has short graying hair that is wild, barely clipped down into a pair of sparkly barrettes. Her shoulders sag with the weight of age and sadness. I think of how much my formerly tall, powerful mother looks like a child in this moment, and in a strange way I feel glad for it.

"Not so good, honey," Mom replies, her voice wavering. "Gran-Gran hasn't been conscious in days. We don't know if she's brain-dead or not. They want us to put her on a feeding tube, but the family all decided against it. We're just waiting..." she trails off, unable to speak the inevitable.

I take a breath and struggle for a response. I've always been terrible at moments like this. I feel sure that there must be a correct response—maybe crying, hugging, or expressing my own grief to share in the burden, but I have no comfort to offer. Instead I answer with what I hope feels like sympathetic silence.

We drive straight from the airport to the hospital. Normally our first hour together would be filled with Mom's happy interrogations: *Tell me something wonderful about the kids. How is Brett these days? Are you still liking your job? How are the kids doing in school?* But on this night there is only cold and darkness between us.

I roll my carry-on bag across the snow-covered parking lot and follow Mom through the lobby and up the elevator. We cross the hall and enter the room where my grandmother lies in final sleep. As I approach her bed, I lay my young hand on her old one. *Children and the dying*, I ponder, *they are the only ones who can touch me.* She looks to me now as she always has, always the same, even when I had become her granddaughter twenty-eight years earlier—small, ancient, timeless with her immense hair pulled into a bun at the top of her head.

Mom's sister Gail and Gail's daughter Angela kept bedside vigil while Mom went to the airport. Now they stand and we trade mournful hugs. We murmur a quick conversation, *Hello, so good to see you, so glad you are here*, and then I assume my post beside Gran-Gran's bed. This is the unspoken arrangement: that I will keep watch over her so all the others can sleep. Everyone goes home to rest.

Once alone, I take a seat and pull out the novel I started on the flight, *Water for Elephants*. As I leaf toward my bookmarked page, I notice a corkboard mounted on the wall across from me. It is just inside the room's entrance, so I hadn't noticed it earlier. On that corkboard are pinned sheets of white paper, and on those papers are printed old photographs. I move to take a closer look. They are photos of my grandmother from her youth, taken before she became Gran-Gran, Grandma, Momma, or even Mrs. Blake. These sepia-toned prints are simply Elizabeth McPherson before she had loved a man named Billy Blake and sent him off to the Great War. I search her small, bright eyes for a sign of the five children, twelve grandchildren, or twelve great-grandchildren to come, but they reveal no secrets. Young Liz McPherson had not yet waited out a war or buried a husband and a son. She stands arm in arm with her friends, their skirts billowing in an unseen breeze, laughing over a joke long since dissolved.

I gaze from the youthful photos to her tired body on the bed, and I feel an unfamiliar but undeniable pull of familial love. This feeling is like a stranger to me. It has something to do with comprehending the whole of a person, in knowing him or her as more than just the person that stands before you. That is the way I love my children; I can never see or love just one moment of them, for I am always seeing every moment of them, everything that came before and might come after. Each child is an infinite collage of warm sleeping breath, worrisome fever, sloppy open-mouthed kiss, victorious step, painstaking Mother's Day gift, silly dance, and butterfly kiss. My maternal love does not brush across them like a paint stroke; it envelopes the whole of them like murals of the Sistine Chapel.

Strange to feel chords of that enveloping love for someone other than my children—for my grandmother, whom I am just now learning to really see.

Do I love her because I know her? Or do I know her because I love her? Must one precede the other?

Do we love others because they're ours, or are they ours because we love each other? Which creates the family?

I return to the stiff hospital chair and my book. In it, I read Jacob's parallel plot of youth, age, and all that comes between as I simultaneously process my grandmother's own youth, age, and now death.

Later I find out that my Aunt Sandy posted those photos in hopes that they'd have a similar effect on the nurses as they have on me—that we not see an old lady at the end of her life, but a whole person who had once been beautiful outside and remains so inside.

We go on for a few days, taking shifts at her bedside, grabbing short bouts of sleep, holding our quiet, hopeless vigil. We watch the gentle snow from the hospital window—the whites of its days and blacks of its nights. We hear a rattle in Gran-Gran's chest amplify as her lungs slowly fill with fluid.

Then one night, the hospital staff tells us that Gran-Gran will be moved to hospice. There is nothing more they can do. Her daughters and granddaughters weep. They come to terms with the fact. As the staff prepares her to move, Gran-Gran's breathing grows alarmingly loud as her lungs fill completely. The machinery sings its alert— *Prepare! Prepare!* We watch her drown silently in a soft hospital bed, in a sea of her daughters' tears. She will not be going to hospice after all, for in these final, dramatic moments, Gran-Gran makes her way out of this world.

The room explodes in sorrow. Family members are suddenly everywhere, gasping sobs, holding each other up, falling down from the grief of losing their mother and grandmother. Mom collapses on Gran-Gran's bed, draped over her body, wracked with heaving sobs. Over and over again, she wails, "Oh, Momma! Momma!"

I stand in the midst of this chaos but observe as if I am standing behind a glass wall. I feel a tremendous sadness but not grief. I have loved Gran-Gran in my own way, and I have admired her greatly, but I do not feel an urge to mourn. She is simply gone, just as everyone leaves, and what does it matter how they leave us—in dying or walking away, either way they are gone. I wonder if my lack of mourning and comfort make me a little inhuman.

After a short time that must have felt like ages to Mom, she stands and wipes her eyes. She walks over to me, spent from those first moments of raw grief, and in her need for physical comfort, she reaches to hug me. There we stand for a few moments, not as replacement mother and replacement daughter, but simply as two women who both know the loss of mother—she, immersed in her despair, and I behind my wall of glass.

Ancient Wounds

Omma's letter, May 4, 2014

    After that, my life was hard. I could not pay my rent, so I was homeless when I gave birth. I slept here and there, and my kidnapper had a basement room, so I went to him with my baby. I became normalized as I raised my baby. As long as the kidnapper gave me money, I could live. But he became drunk more and more, and even beat me sometimes. My baby was growing but without a name or family registration. I felt that I had to do something about it, but I could not. He did not come home for many days. Then, when he came home, he gave me some money. Already one year passed like this, and I made up my mind to do something. I tried to find his relatives, but no one knew about him. I was looking for a babysitter and tried to earn money, but I could not find a babysitter. One day I found him at the street. He was dead on the street. I was in such shock. It seemed he just died as a heavy alcoholic. Then I asked my sister to look after my baby, as I needed to earn money. My sister said yes. I worked hard but could not make enough money to get a room.

*****

Spring 2008

    Ideas begin as less than a whisper of a thought. They are like those first few cells deep inside a woman's core—hardly a real thing but already ripe with potential. Those idea cells gather momentum and travel to the front of our consciousness, building strength and substance along the way. We conceive and give birth to ideas like they are our progeny.

    It is springtime in 2008, and I am pregnant with one

big idea: adopting a child. I don't know why or how I pick up this notion, but once I do there is no putting it down. Once the idea becomes fully formed and planted in my mind, I begin researching the process. The first order of business, before I get too carried away, is to get Brett's agreement.

"Uh, Brett? I was wondering, I mean, I have an idea, and kinda wanna see what you think about it."

"Cool, what's up?"

"Hmm, well, I've been thinking, you know, I think we're pretty okay with the kids and with three we're already playing zone defense, and you know I *never* want to be pregnant again, but I feel like we could have another kid. I mean, we *could* adopt one. I think that would be good. What do you think?"

"Cool, sure. Why not?"

And just like that, we decide to adopt our fourth child.

We ask ourselves all the typical questions: How much will it cost? Should we adopt domestically or internationally? What about Korea? What are all the requirements and can we manage them? We embark on the adoption process as ignorant and naïve as tourists.

Finally, through the process of elimination, we settle on adoption from China. Our reasons are like so many other American families who choose Chinese adoption: China is easy. The industry that collects Chinese daughters and sends them to the US is huge and efficient. It is well supported and therefore streamlined and unintimidating. In classic *Freakonomics* terms, we are, quite simply, incentivized to select Chinese adoption.

Most importantly, from China we have access to an abundant supply of "waiting children." We don't bother reflecting on the root causes of why these children are waiting and what we might do about that. Like many families who adopt, we're not interested in sending our

$30,000 to a country in need without getting something to show for our generosity. We're in it for ourselves.

Once we select our country, we settle on Holt International as our agency. By this time we live in Florida, and Holt has a strong presence there. In fact, Holt has a strong presence everywhere. Holt is the megalopolis of all international adoption agencies, having invented the industry during the post-Korean War years. "Grandma" Bertha Holt raised six biological children and then, after the age of fifty, went on to adopt eight more from Korea. She was an indomitable woman, literally impelling an act of Congress to allow her family to adopt so many children internationally. Bertha Holt then went on to open the floodgate that would, to date, send more than two hundred thousand children away from Korea and eventually countless more from other places like China, India, and South America.

On August 15, 2008, I formally submit our online application and $200 application fee. The wheel begins its revolution.

Our family goes through the machinations of the adoption process. We break the news of our decision, first to our three children and then to the rest of our families. We slog through months of home studies and adoption classes. I compulsively stalk countless online forums and the Waiting Child list, where we window-shop the little photos like they are furniture. We wait anxiously to be matched with a child.

In March 2009, I get the big call.

"Hello, this is Raina."

"Hello! This is Nicole from Holt International! I'm calling to let you know we have a match! Do you have a few minutes to talk?"

Does a bear shit in the woods? "Really? Yes, of course."

"Great! First let me explain how this will work! I'll

give you all the details now over the phone, and then I'll email some documents to you! They'll be the child's complete file from China, including medical and developmental history, some info about the orphanage, stuff like that! We'll also include an example of the Letter of Intent that you'll need to fill out if you want to move forward with this match! Sound good?" Nicole is mighty perky.

I grunt the equivalent of a blank, uncomprehending nod. I didn't expect to get matched so quickly.

Nicole proceeds to run down all the pertinent information. We have been matched with a little girl; her name is Zhan Ai Na, she is almost six years old, she lives in Guangdong province. Nicole also gives me a brief overview of Ai Na's medical history and some personality descriptions that the orphanage provided.

Moments after our conversation, Nicole sends the email: "Dear Brett and Raina, Congratulations on your referral! Here is the child information Zhan Ai Na! The photos of this lovely child are included in the PDF." Nicole's email outlines the next five-hundred steps required for us to officially accept our referral, and includes about seven-hundred attachments (or maybe just thirteen).

I am both stunned and thrilled. This child will be second in age-order with our others. Malia has just turned seven, and the boys are both under five. After some quick discussions with Brett and our pediatrician, we make our decision: Zhan Ai Na will be our little girl.

*****

If my year in Korea illuminated some of my scars, and if becoming a mother started to scratch at them, then entering the adoption process rips those ancient wounds wide open inside me. I bleed.

I study up on how to be a good American adopter. I learn about the grief that my daughter will suffer, and I break into my own unacknowledged grief. I study the challenges she will have establishing her racial and cultural identity in a transnational family, and I tear into my own latent loneliness and confusion. The more I build myself as an adoptive parent, the more broken I become as an adopted person.

To further complicate things, the biological mother in me starts to think differently. In her view, the abandonment story is a load of shit. Now that I have given birth to children, the notion that a mother would relinquish her child out of love just doesn't add up. I find myself contemplating what other forces could have been at work and the devastation my own Korean mother must have endured. Instead of just wondering about my Korean mother from a daughter's perspective, I begin to empathize with her as a fellow mother.

*****

I am reading *A Thousand Splendid Suns.* In the streets of Kabul, amid the brutality of the Taliban and the oppression of extremist Muslim culture, I have taken a mental and spiritual journey with two women: Mariam and Laila. The violence, inequities, and utter disregard for an entire gender are shocking. Even more stunning for me is that this novel, which speaks so clearly to my soul as a mother and free women, was written by a man. How could Khaled Hosseni know the depths of a mother's love and pain? How can he understand the infinite capacity mothers have to hope, to endure for the sake of their children?

It is rare that a novel will bring tears to my eyes. When Laila relinquishes her daughter to an orphanage, where she will receive food and clothing that her own poverty-stricken family can no longer provide, it is unbearable. Her loss is my own as I imagine how squalid life would have to become for me to hand my own lovely Malia over "for her own good." That very idea has me shaking inside. My eyes sting and my soul churns at the mere notion of leaving my daughter, whatever the circumstance.

My whole life, I have framed the world through the lens of an adoptee: a child who was abandoned by one family, claimed by another. I have been told I was a toddler wandering the streets of Seoul, name pinned to my shirt—an orphan, malnourished and dirty. Then I became a prize smothered in love by my American family. When Malia was born, I added the lens of a mother's perspective. As a mother, I finally understood the infinite reach of a mother's love. These children are the most important, best work of my life, just as I was for my mother before me.

And now, a new type of motherhood is coming into focus. My final child still slumbers on a cot half the world away, oblivious to the tremors and quakes in her future. She goes on through her routine, unaware that a mother on this side of the earth dreams of Chinese girls and the women who abandon them. I am now beginning to comprehend the horrors another mother faced years ago—pinning a child's name and birthday to her shirt, pinning all hopes for that child's life in the hands of fate.

I grieve not only for the orphaned children, robbed of their childhoods. But I also mourn the women who still feel their children in their arms, like phantom limbs leaving only pain where vitality once was. The mothers who will never know what became of their babies, will never know if their decision was correct, will never find peace or resolution. In waking hours, they must convince themselves their darlings are now safe, grown, successful. But in night's unguarded hours, surely they suffer the realization of every parent's worst fears. I imagine that abandoning one's child must be pure hell on earth.

There is a common fantasy involved with international adoption: The poverty-stricken family. The beloved infant gently swaddled, then surreptitiously left on the steps of the orphanage. The longing backward glance, and a dream of a better life. Watch any Hollywood movie, it's always done the same way.

That is the fantasy I believed all through my childhood. Although my mother had told me that I was abandoned at the age of eighteen months, that had always translated into the swaddled-baby version of the story. Not until I had a daughter of my own did I fully understand that I had been no gurgling bundle of joy when my parents cut me loose; I was a full-blown little person.

I discovered, to my delight and surprise, my Malia could do so many things at eighteen months old. She could sing, count, run, laugh hard, give butterfly kisses, say "I love you, Mommy." When my husband and I deployed to Iraq and she went to live with my sister, she wiped away my tears and told me "It be okay, Mommy." At eighteen months old!

I also know what parenting a child for eighteen months does to a person. You are familiar with every nook and cranny of baby flesh. You have nurtured, protected, cleaned, and worried over this tiny person with all your heart and soul. So much of you is inextricably tied to this child, you are merely fragments in her absence.

It is with this new insight that I have revised my understanding of my own abandonment. It stings to think that my parents did know me, maybe even loved me, for over a year before relinquishing me to fate. One wonders how parents could make a decision to parent for a year and then walk away. Was it too difficult? Was it just not worth the effort? Did they feel regret or merely relief? Do they still remember the games we played, the kisses we exchanged, the songs we sang? Can they remember the sound of my voice, of my cries? Do they miss me?

And I feel so much sadness for that child, who was suddenly all alone. I can see her wandering the streets, looking, searching, never finding. I am utterly sick over her loss.

*****

The adoption process creates in me an obsessive mania. We navigate through a mountain of paperwork that is known in the adoption community as a "paper chase." I don't know if the connotation suggests that we are chasing our way through a paperwork race, and the prize at the finish line is a child? Or does it imply that we are constantly being chased by this headless, heartless monster of paperwork. It feels like both, for the amount of documentation, validation, and certification in adoption makes getting a mortgage feel like the Dumbo ride at Disney World.

The process of adopting from China is strenuous, and for a time I become more focused on the getting of our child than the ultimate parenting of her. Adoption becomes alarmingly tantamount to acquisition.

I selfishly bemoan the wait, the complications, the delays, the expenses that stand between us and the child I now feel entitled to. How dare the Chinese and US governments put so many constraints on this process! How unfair that we should be forced to wait for a child, fill out so much paperwork, be subject to so much inconsistency in the process.

The wait is difficult, and it is easiest to see it from only the adopter's side. But there is someone else to consider—while my wait might feel agonizing, our daughter has a viewpoint of her own. She is six years old. She has friends, nannies, and teachers; she has grown well and consistently. For her, the real tribulations will begin when we arrive in China to upend her life. We will be her problem before we can be a solution. I feel sorry for all that we are about to put our sweet daughter through.

As we inch closer to our official travel approval from the Chinese government, which is the final hurdle before booking a flight to meet our child and bring her home, I think ahead. I've heard the term "Gotcha Day" used to describe the day when families meet their adopted children, and I find it puzzling and problematic. It occurs to me that adopted children do not, in fact, want to be gotten. If they had their way, most would choose to never have been lost in the first place. While we wait for our daughter, I increasingly feel suspended between two adoptions. Two losses. There is a Prufrockian room in my mind where birth mothers, lost children, adoptive mothers, and adopted children all commune together. They make introductions, trade old stories, and come to realize that they are all reflections of each other.

Her Alien Language

Omma's letter, May 4, 2014

One summer day, my sister's husband went bankrupt, so they became nearly homeless. So I brought back my baby and looked for a job while I carried my baby on my back. Then someone told me that I could temporarily leave my baby at a facility. I thought that it would be okay as long as my baby was okay. So I left my baby at a facility near to Noryangjin police station to get a job. But I could not earn enough money. I always lived in poverty, no matter how hard I worked.

Often I went to the facility to see my baby. The first few times, the owner of the facility welcomed me, as I took the baby clothes. Then they began to treat me harshly. Then they told me "Don't come often" and even "Do not come at all," as my visit would make my baby confused. Nevertheless, I visited the facility to see my baby, but the owner of the facility began to get angry with me. Whenever I visited my baby, the owner told me, "You are a penniless single mom, so if you raise the baby, the baby will be unhappy." The owner persuaded me to send away my baby for overseas adoption to the USA, saying my baby would grow up happily with a rich American family.

My baby entered the facility on August 7, 1978, and then in July or August 1979, I gave approval for my baby to be sent overseas for adoption. Then thirty-four years passed. I read my letters to my child many times, and I felt so sorry to my child. I could feel that my child was so lonely. I felt so sorry to my child. No words can express my feeling of loss during the last thirty-four years.

*****

Winter 2009

In November we receive our final approval from the Chinese government to travel to China, and on December 3, Malia and I embark on our journey halfway around the world. Two are leaving, three will return.

We liftoff from JAX en route to EWR, where we link up with Brett's aunt Laurie who agreed to be my sherpa. From there, the three of us make a direct flight over the Arctic Circle from EWR to PEK. Total travel time: twenty hours.

Malia is the only child on the plane, and she is a rock star. I've never traveled internationally with a seven-year-old and don't know what to expect. Nor have I spent much time with Laurie, but she has a family reputation for not traveling well. Thankfully, I don't notice this at all—perhaps the happy drugs and four Jack & Cokes do the trick. On this flight I don't know who I am more proud of, Malia or Aunt Laurie.

We fly on a Boeing 777 aircraft with Continental Airlines. It's quite comfortable, and the amenities are worth every dime of the economy airfare. Each seat has its own entertainment center with a touch screen, game controller, and a full library of movies, TV shows, and games. I practice some Mandarin on one of the games but can't seem to get any further than "I don't understand." An animated map tracks our flight progress along with a lot of useful data like ground speed, distance traveled, times in the departing and destination cities, and outside temperature, which is my favorite, as I watch it dip down to -81degrees Fahrenheit somewhere over Siberia.

Our plane's route travels over Canada, Greenland, the Arctic Circle, Siberia, and Inner Mongolia. *If we crash*, I think to myself as Laurie and Malia doze, *I hope we go out in a ball of flames. It's too damn cold down there to try to survive.*

We deplane at Terminal 3 of PEK. If you've never

seen the Beijing airport, it is massive, sleek, and suspiciously clean. The immigration and health officials all wear SARS masks, and the process of clearing customs and immigration is hushed and efficient.

We make our way out of the concourse and find our guide waiting by the exit doors. He holds one of those signs with my name printed on it—I feel so important! We load into the van and careen to our hotel in downtown Beijing.

Our first full day in Beijing starts at 3a.m., not because we have anything to do but because we can't sleep any longer. We meet two other adopting families at breakfast; apparently Holt cranks a lot of families through this hotel. The breakfast buffet is a two-hour extravaganza of dumplings, egg rolls, baked tomatoes, sushi, watermelon, salad, crepes, lo mein, and broiled fish. We finally head back to the room to put on every layer we can find and meet our guide, Tina, in the lobby.

Tina is an adorable student who has a funny way of explaining things fast and then repeating them slow, like maybe we didn't catch it the first time. She is native to Beijing, and you can tell just how proud she is of her city. Tina has much to be proud of—fifteen million people and about a century of progress in the 40 years since the Cultural Revolution.

We have only a few days in Beijing. In that time we trek the Badaling section of the Great Wall and tour a cloisonné factory. We ride pedicab rickshaws through Hutong Alley, where a beautiful, timeless woman invites us for tea in the ancient courtyard of her Hutong home. She touches Malia's face and marvels over her "talking eyes." We tour Tiananmen Square and the Forbidden City, where I have a comical case of mistaken identity when the security staff assumes I am a Chinese citizen sneaking in with the group of American tourists. We wander the hushed aisles of Beijing's largest bookstore. We explore the open-air vendors of "snack street," a showcase of exotic delicacies: sea snakes, sheep's penis, starfish, bee cocoons, centipedes, and many more that we can't even guess at.

Our brief time in Beijing is a whirlwind journey across time and culture, but I am nearly too distracted to take much of it in. We are here on a mission to adopt, and in some ways the pageantry of Beijing is just an obstacle between us and our objective.

*****

We leave the White Swan in Guangzhou at 2p.m.and arrive at the room where we will meet our children. I take a picture of the room's name so I will always remember the place where we first met: Adoption Registry Center of Guangdong Province.

There are thirty-nine families in total, but it feels more like one hundred thirty-nine. Some families already have their children, most are still waiting. Children filter in at random intervals through one door. It is highly informal, and nothing at all what I expected. I watch this door and wait impassively. I was expecting to feel something in this moment, but I am numb, cold, and calm. It's a typical response in emotionally charged situations, and once again I think my emotion maker must be broken. I take cues from the other parents—how to be excited and happy. I watch their reactions as they meet their new children so I can display similarly appropriate behavior. But inside, there is nothing for me.

A couple other Holt families have their children now, so I am occupied with taking their pictures and videos. Someone catches my attention, urges me to turn around, and suddenly there she is—the child from my referral photos. She is a vision in corduroy, head to toe, and my first thought is "HOLY PINK."Her brightly embroidered black pants are about two inches too short, and her electric pink coat is an inch too short in the arms and buttoned all the way up to her neck. It's way too hot in here for a coat, and I wonder how she can bear the oppression of the heat and the anxiety. Her socks are orange and green, adorned with knock-off Winnie the Pooh and Piglet characters. Over those she wears pink and white sneakers, about three sizes too large and also brand-new. Her hair is cropped short, with bangs cut straight across and a hair clip pulling them directly to the side. She carries a small water bottle, a pink plastic comb, and the four-by-six photo album we sent her months ago. She shuffles toward us now, and while I stand there stupidly trying to imitate the joy of all the parents around me, Malia steps in as ambassador and peacemaker.

Later, in the retelling of this scene, I will tell friends and family that I fell in love on first sight. But in this moment, there is only a scared mom and child carefully playing off each other, move-countermove, like a bizarre chess match where fear and loss are pawns and acceptance is queen.

Between the two of us, Maia—that will be her new name—is the first to crack. Her narrow chin quivers and a tear slides down her cheek. She is trying so hard to be brave, but she's just a little girl in the most terrifying moment of her life.

I have little comfort to offer, and it's Laurie who makes the big breakthrough. She's not bogged down with the heavy task of pretending to be a normally functioning mother; she still has her wits about her. Laurie walks over to a vending machine and returns with an icy cold Coca-Cola. Like every parent since the beginning of time, we bribe our child with sweets.

It's time to leave now. We all board the bus that takes us to the White Swan Hotel on Shamian Island. Maia sits next to me, clutching her Coca-Cola and her apprehension. She stares out the window, and after a few minutes she reaches over to hold my hand. Checkmate.

*****

The rest of our time in China is spent on the typical adoption activities. It's a weeklong sleepwalk through government offices, medical exams, and tourist activities. Four of us are crammed into a tiny hotel room and between the few official activities, we have a lot of time to kill. Within this extraordinary experience in a magnificent foreign country, we are mired in a boredom dotted with remarkable moments: watching Aunt Laurie get mobbed by the Chinese who are fascinated with her blonde hair, Maia's first kisses, riding elephants, small conversations between my daughters.

By the time we board the first of several planes to make our way back home, we are ready to get back to our normal lives. It takes thirty-six hours to make the trip back to Florida where we are finally, completely, irreversibly, a family of six.

*****

The following year is the hardest year of my adult life. Oh, I've had worse years, like the time I got kicked out of West Point for underage drinking (I did eventually earn my way back in and graduate). I've had more eventful years, like the time my husband was deployed to Iraq while I parented our toddler and gave birth to our second child. But nothing has come close to the stress of holding our family together through the adoption of an older child, the induction of a slightly insane Chinese au pair, the slow death of my husband's career, and my own awakening to the grief of abandonment and adoption.

Our au pair, Huan, arrives the day before we return

from Guangzhou. She seems nice enough, but that's because we don't yet realize that her brand of crazy operates in stealth mode.

We selected Huan as our au pair for her Cantonese language skills, which she had highlighted on her resume and we had specifically required during the interview process. Our logic was that a Chinese au pair would help our newly integrated daughter make the transition from Chinese orphanage to American family. She could act as translator between Maia and us, and she could help us learn some Cantonese. Most importantly, she could offer safety instructions and warnings in Cantonese language for those dangerous moments—like running across the street or sticking a fork in the power outlet—when there simply wouldn't be time for translation.

I couldn't be more thrilled that we had found such an ingenious parenting solution to the practical challenge of language. We were already such clever adoptive parents, and we hadn't even started yet!

Clever, that is, until the first red flag shoots up like a dandelion in a perfectly manicured lawn. She can't speak Cantonese. We don't learn this right away because Huan does speak a few words here and there. She speaks enough to get Maia's attention, but when we press her to translate, she acts confused. After a week, Huan finally admits she is not fluent. Maia speaks only Cantonese. We speak only English. Our failure of a translator speaks only Mandarin.

I rationalize that the language "misunderstanding" is not such a big deal. With both Brett and I working full time, it will be a huge undertaking to go through the process of replacing Huan with a new au pair, not to mention the disruption that our kids–especially Maia–would experience with yet another switch in childcare. We will have to find a way to make it work.

The thing about dandelions is they don't show up alone. The first one is a scout. Once that bright, yellow, kind-of-cute little flower takes root, it invites its family of twelve hundred other dandelions, and soon they are like a virus spreading across your lawn.

Huan's next dandelion springs up one night as the kids are getting ready for bed. I am in the kitchen slicing a mango. Cade, who is three years old now, calls me for help, so I rest my knife and uneaten mango on the cutting board to check on him. As I help him dress into his pajamas, I hear an odd, worried muttering from the kitchen. Next I hear the sound of quick footsteps from the kitchen to the kids' bathroom, which is immediately adjacent to his bedroom. These sounds all pass within a few seconds of each other, and I don't really pay attention until I hear a loud *thud* against the wall between Cade's room and the bathroom.

What the hell?

I finish pulling his shirt over his head and peer out his bedroom door to see if the others are okay. I am expecting to see a child with a dropped toy or a dining chair accidentally knocked over. What I do see are a pair of long legs laying on the bathroom floor with their homemade house slippers protruding out the door. I rush out and, turning the corner into the bathroom, I find Huan sprawled ungraciously across the floor with a paper towel wrapped around her finger. Nanny down! I quickly kneel on the floor to revive her before the children notice that anything is awry.

I gently shake her shoulder and prod in a low voice, "Huan, what happened? Get up."

No luck.

Raising my voice, I urge, "Huan, I need you to get up! The kids are coming!"

Still completely knocked out.

By this time the kids, with their uncanny ability to only be able to hear my voice when I'm trying to keep it from them, have sensed that something really fun and exciting must be happening in the bathroom. They rush to partake in the festivities.

I move into a full-blown scream with equally violent shaking, "HUAN, I NEED YOU TO BE AN ADULT AND GET UP OFF THE FLOOR. YOU ARE SCARING THE CHILDREN!"

About the time I finish screaming and shaking her, Ty starts singing with delight "Huan's dead! Huan's dead!" as Cade kicks her in the solar plexus. The chorus of my desperate screams, Ty's gleeful chants, and Cade's tiny kicks finally rouse her from peaceful slumber.

"Oh oh!" She mumbles. Her eyes flutter open and she struggles to sit up. "Oh, I cut my finger."

Well shit. She passes out at the sight of blood.

After several minutes, Huan becomes sufficiently lucid for me to interrogate without feeling like a totally unsympathetic ass (which I was), and we have time to explore the issue. No, this isn't a common occurrence. Yes, it's happened once before. No, not with other people's blood, only her own.

Thus begins the year of au pair misunderstandings and misadventures.

*****

Spring 2010

Maia feels like an invader in my home. I have been a mother for almost eight years already—a mother to three children carried in my womb, born of my flesh, nurtured and fed from my body and carrying my DNA. These spectacular children look just like me. I understand every nuance of their voice intonations, of their vast variety of facial expressions. I can decode each cry and decipher each whimper. I have fussed over every last dimple and pudge. I have trimmed those sixty fingers and toenails, brushed those thousands of hairs, shared those infinite smiles. My babies have survived earaches, stomach viruses, stitches, scabies, Fifth disease, nosebleeds, and all types of emergency room mishaps. These children are my people–my only biological people–and our short history is sacred to me.

Then along comes our Maia. She is an alien-child, brought into our home at age six with her own peculiar customs and separate set of genes. She has shared her history with others, and there is no re-writing of it. Her alien planet is enigmatic; her ways are strange. She climbs up and down the walls, attacks us with unfettered affection, and rages with confusion and grief. She is darling and wonderful, frightened and frightening. She is still a stranger in our house.

Day by day, we learn each other. She senses my frustration and eventually sees that it is nothing to fear. I sense her loss and struggle to find courage to fill it. She slowly, over time, realizes that I am for real. We are on a strange, scary path toward each other, and we both understand that while there is so much to gain, there is also so much at risk. It is easy to say the words "I love you," but much harder to fulfill those words.

On a regular Saturday night about four months after Maia joins our family, I find her crying alone in her room. She holds photos of herself and friends from the orphanage, photos that the orphanage had sent to us shortly before we traveled to China. Here is a photo of a field trip they took to McDonald's in Zhanjiang. Here is a photo of her and some friends doing full splits in gymnastics class. These are some of the last memories she has of the home and faces she had known her whole life. Quiet tears slide down her cheeks.

I sit in the floor next to Maia and place my arm around her. We sit like that, not speaking, just watching as she silently flips through each photo, examining the life she had left behind. For a fleeting moment, I worry that our family will not be enough to fill the emptiness of all she had lost. I wonder, only for a moment, if we had truly done what was best for her by taking her from a life she had loved. In the next moment, I reaffirm to myself that it is within my power to make it the best for her. Friends are not enough to sustain a child. Caregivers cannot truly nurture a child. Only a family can truly sustain and nurture. It's hard to know the right way to parent this alien-child, but it is crucial that we do so.

Despite my uncertainty, a deep down part of me— one that had also been lost long ago—speaks her alien language. Our stories are both written in common landscapes, of mothers lost and families found. Although Maia and I don't share a biological history, we share history of a different type. We have our own kind of mutual DNA. We were once citizens of the same lost planet.

****

Summer 2010

Reflections on these first few months as Maia's mom. Early on, she was constantly greeting us. "Hi Mommy!" "Hi Daddy!" We must have heard that fifty times a day until she realized it was only necessary for initial meetings. She did not know how to pucker for kisses. Once learned, she wanted to kiss on the mouth over and over again, for extend periods of time. I would push her away, laughing "We don't need to make out!" Now she has learned the normal ways to hug and kiss family.

At first, Maia clearly associated family love with being a "good child." She always wanted to seem perfect. She lied. She blamed her siblings. She went into terrified rages when she was caught doing something wrong.

She's still learning to trust us—to know that we will still love her when she makes mistakes. She's still practicing how to be authentic to herself, rather than perfect for us.

She continues to have a peculiar way of being disappointed with our life. She constantly tells me what she doesn't have. Seeing another child's toy, she'll complain she doesn't have one too. Seeing a bigger, fancier house, she'll tell the owner theirs is better than ours. At the store, she expects me to buy everything. She is shockingly wasteful. She breaks things constantly. Sometimes she'll take one bite of an apple and throw the rest away. We are not a wasteful family, nor are we rich. She seems to be highly disappointed about that.

One of my first impressions of Maia was how skinny but tough she was, and she continues to surprise me in this way. She is amazingly strong for her size, but still lacks body awareness. She still falls out of the bed, falls out of chairs, falls down when just walking across the room. Of the components of physical ability, she rates high on strength, endurance, and flexibility. It is coordination that she is lacking, but she makes up for it in enthusiasm!

Her first trip to the pool was in April. She tried to imitate the swimming motions of the other kids but could only manage to flop her upper body around in a really embarrassing way. Her compact muscular body does not float. But by May, she was diving underwater and swimming like an adorable little dolphin. She can't get enough of the pool these days, and fortunately we live in a climate that allows outdoor swimming eight months out of the year.

After one month, she could follow verbal instructions with no gesturing. By two months, she could have a rudimentary conversation. Now we are developing her phonemic awareness through "Hooked on Phonics," and she is finally starting to understand the structure of our language. We need to teach her to read soon. Thankfully, she still doesn't understand sarcasm because sometimes I can't restrain myself. I wonder if she will lose her thick Cantonese accent.

Her hair is finally growing into a bob. As soon as it got long enough to reach her mouth, Maia started sucking on her hair. After three separate warnings that I would cut her hair if she didn't stop, I finally trimmed it up. She howled for hours after that trim, sobbing over and over "I don't want to cut my hair." I felt like a wicked witch.

We are still working hard to teach her about discipline and honesty. She is less dependent now on her orphanage survival skills and more in tune to the patterns of family. She has a generous spirit and a very poorly developed sense of ownership and responsibility. If one of the other kids lets her play with something, she believes she owns it. If they want something of hers, she gives it to them. She spends all her birthday money on her siblings.

There is a lot of fighting and frustration among the kids.

But my girls, they act like true sisters. They could not be better playmates, and they adore each other when they don't "hate" each other. Hearing their laughter, seeing them choose matching outfits, makes my heart happy. These two girls will be co-conspirators through life. It means the world to me that they have each other. My boys, they just go with the flow. Maia is just another big sister to them: someone else to boss them around, get on their nerves, help when they need it.

We have come a long way, and have a long way yet to go. I struggle with this. For me, becoming a parent to an older adopted child is not the same as becoming a parent to a newborn biologically related infant. How could it be? We don't have the physical connection. We both entered this relationship with well-formed personalities and opinions. We spend a lot of time trying to please each other, and yet mold each other to our own design. We're still learning of each other and, most importantly, learning to trust one another.

Maia was completely dependent on me long before she knew, loved, or trusted me. The need is always there; the other feelings are still forming. We are still half-strangers. I want to be a better mother to this extraordinary child. I am only human, though. I have little patience and am always tired. I think she is a better daughter than I am a mother, but we are family now.

*****

One night about five months after joining our family, Maia talks to me about her happy memories of China for the first time. This is amazing on so many levels.

First, the fact that she is talking, mostly in English, mostly coherently, and somewhat in sentences. Second, that she is old enough to have memories of her motherland, and old enough to communicate them. These are memories that, if nurtured, will stay with her forever. She'll always know who she is, where she came from. How I wish I had such memories of my prior life. Third, that her memories are happy. She cries out in joy at photos of her social welfare institute (SWI), her *ayi* nannies (one of whom she loves), her friends. Her life. She was happy there, and she is happy here. Fourth, that she is telling all of this to me. She trusts me. She wants to share her happiness with me.

Clearly she loved her life in China. She talks cheerfully about returning to China, taking gifts to her nannies, someday attending her former school again, and reuniting with her "sisters" and "brothers." She asks to be called by her Chinese name, and so we sometimes call her Ai Na, sometimes Maia.

At the beginning of this conversation, though, my protective reflex kicks in. My first instinct is a fear that she loves her Chinese life more than this one, that she wants those children in the SWI to be her sisters and brothers again. With those words, for just a moment, Maia knocks the wind out of me. This is not a safe place for either of us. I am too much like a child, still afraid of rejection.

I suppose these are normal feelings of parenting, especially in adoption: threatened when our child longs for something other than what we can provide, discouraged when what we offer doesn't seem good enough. But as parents, that is when we have to tighten our focus and remind ourselves–this parenting gig is not about us. It is about our children, preparing them to be secure, happy, and productive adults. Advocating for them in whatever ways we are required.

Of all people, I should know better. I let a defensive parenting response rise in my heart for a wavering moment. Then, thankfully, my experience as an adoptee and mother to three other children kicks in, and I do what any good parent should when their child begins to open up: I shut my mouth, listen, and remember that—as in nearly everything in life—it's not about me.

As a result, I am rewarded with stories about her days in the SWI: the sleeping arrangements, the school, her nannies and teachers, the clothes, food, friends. I listen to Maia recount her happy memories of China–not "mommy's China" in Guangzhou and Beijing, but the SWI, which she endearingly calls "my China." I do my best to affirm all these extraordinarily valid feelings of hers.

For a night, we lie on the floor talking and listening, and Maia moves a little closer to wholeness. It might be further away from me, or closer to me, but the point is this: my location is of no consequence to her wholeness. I will always move closer to her. My children—none of them—belong to me. But I will always belong to them, no matter where they go.

*****

Through this year, I experience a growth that ends up being a necessary precursor to the unknown events that will soon unfold. Adopting Maia launches my education about attachment, the "primal wound," and the many ethical problems of today's adoption industry. The more engaged I become, the more I learn. The more I learn, the more I challenge everything I believe about my own history.

As my children's interest in superheroes, princesses, and children's fantasy grow, I notice a trend. The central conflict of most of these stories originates in the same place: the loss of one's parents. Would Superman, Spider-Man, Batman, Iron Man, Captain America, Wolverine, or even Harry Potter have developed their powers or taken up their causes if they hadn't tragically, and often violently, lost their parents at a young age? If comic book tales and fantasy literature are a modern version of American mythology, then this pattern indicates our collective acknowledgement that the most galvanizing and enduring–indeed, transforming–trauma that a person can survive is the loss of one's parents. How much more shocking, then, that we live in a world that would intentionally create this loss through an industry that sometimes strives to serve itself more than the families it was created to serve.

As I stumble through my new adoptive parenthood, I experience the dramatic emotional extremes of my own awakening. I pass through all five stages of grief in this year–grief that has long been suppressed and ignored, fueled by a loss that has never been properly acknowledged or mended.

I stall out in the anger phase for months. My fury grows, morphs, it leaves no survivors. I am furious at the world for allowing the injustice of a mother and child to be separated. I blame God for creating such a world. I resent adoptive parents, including my own, in some ways including myself, for not being equipped to heal the sucking chest wound of losing my first mother. I begrudge America for never fully letting me in, and Korea for rejecting me in the first place. I'm mad at Kim for not feeling the way I do, mad at Brett for not understanding my experience, mad at my kids for being so happy when I am not. Anyone who suggests I should be grateful for the blessings of my life gets a Walter Mitty-esque mental throat punch. I foist my anger without discrimination. My anger spills over to an online blog, where I publicly spew my rage:

I'm going to explain something now, and I really could care less if you understand or not. I'm going to say this, and you can choose to read it, you can close your eyes, you can agree or disagree, and that's it. Just don't argue with me, or try to convince me that I'm wrong because you have absolutely no right to do that to me or anyone else who is smart and brave enough to put ourselves on the line in this type of forum.

For those of you who might be confused as to why adoption bothers adoptees so much, I'm going to give you the short version. When a family walks away from a child, that child loses everything. Have you ever lost EVERYTHING? Every person you know, item you possessed, every feeling of security and happiness – gone without explanation. Do you have a young child? Take that kid to the mall and then leave them there alone. See how they react. Now multiply that times forever.

The earth turns upside down, the sun is black, water

flows uphill and God covers His face in grief.

When children are adopted, especially internationally and transracially, they lose everything again. Only now they not only lose people, things, and security, but they also lose language and all five senses.

We might not remember the loss, but even the knowledge of it is excruciating. Then, some of us grow up to discover that even the remaining shards of our previous memories are but lies. And guess what, it feels a whole lot like losing everything again.

People who have been adopted feel all sorts of different ways about it. We are happy or not. We're sad or not. We're angry or not. We're grateful or not. We're indifferent or not. And every single one of those feelings is perfectly right. We have thoughts about being adopted that are all over the board, and yet every single one of those thoughts is also perfectly right.

There are people who are, at this very minute, talking about adoptees. They're discussing whether we have a right to our opinions and emotions. Whether we should speak out or shut up. There are actually adoptive parents who are debating the pros and cons of listening to the voices of adult adoptees. It makes me want to throw up, then bitch-slap someone, then rescue their children from the willful ignorance in which their whole families will likely drown.

I get it. Everyone experiences loss and grief. Everyone endures tragedy. That's fine—I'll give you yours, and you let me keep mine. I won't judge you for feeling sad about being neglected/abused/etc., and you don't judge me for losing everything in my world three times over. Deal.

I am going to do a search for my birth family, and I want to state right here that if anyone dares to ask me why, prepared to get punched in the ear. 1. It's not your business. 2. If you have to ask the question, you're not going to understand the answer. 3. It's not your business.

Just because I have an awesome life now doesn't mean that I don't have a right to know about my personal history. Stop trying to make me feel like I should get over it. You think you're making me feel better? Go to hell. Take a psychology class. Shut up and listen for once.

And if I want to talk to other adoptees about it and that makes you uncomfortable—you who have lived your whole life surrounded by people who look and smell the same as you, who got homesick the first time you went to summer camp, who have never endured real hunger or coldness, who don't even know what physical discomfort really is—then go away. I don't need you, and you clearly don't need me. We don't have to pretend to like each other. But you leave me and my friends alone.

So there. I feel a little better now... but not much. Because it sickens me to know that so many arrogant, self-righteous, entitled people are still out there teaching their children to be just like them. I feel sorry for them.

For those of you (almost everyone reading this blog) whom I consider friends, family, and allies, I love you all and I'm sorry you had to hear that. At least I managed not to drop any F-bombs today.

*****

Spring 2012

Anger finally subsides and bargaining takes over.

What if I had stayed in Korea? Maybe I would not have felt displaced my whole life.

What if my American family had known better? Maybe I could have adjusted better.

What if I had never become a mother? Maybe I could have stayed in my happy fog of pretending; I could have remained inside the myth of myself.

On a perfect, mild May evening I find myself at the playground watching my younger three children play. Malia is practicing soccer on an adjacent field. The sky is streaked with the glorious oranges and pinks of a Florida sunset, and there's just enough breeze to take the edge off the coming summer humidity. I am emerging from the emotional tumult of the previous two years and starting to feel something close to normalcy and peace. Idyllic moments like this are rare bubbles of quiet happiness, but somehow they feel inexplicably wrong.

Why is it in these moments of serendipity, when my world seems most pure and safe, that I feel most isolated? These moments when I should be happy, instead I find myself guarded against the frailty of it all? I approach these golden days of happiness with a gratitude and fear borne from a primal knowledge of loss. There it is, then: Loss at the core and perimeter of all my perceptions.

It's an emotional homelessness, a perpetual sense of losing, even when all leading indicators show that I am winning. Of course, the reason is because of all I've already lost—family, country, language, name, identity. When your entire identity and life are predicated by loss, then a sense of loss invades and pervades, often in ways that we aren't even aware of. I have spent my early life feeling defective: sad when I should have been happy, grieving something I couldn't even remember and not understanding the nature of that grief, only knowing that the major defining event of my life happened at an age when I internalized without comprehension.

*****

When I emerge from my year of self-loathing, anger, and grief, I began to connect with the idea of my Korean mother. I am convinced that she really is out there, and that she is haunted by the memory of her lost daughter. In a place deeper than my heart, I'm certain she wants me to find her.

I entertain the idea of a search but have no idea where to begin. Mom sends my adoption file, but there is nothing inside but dead ends. I submit my application to appear on an episode of the Korean TV shows "I Miss That Person," which assists with lost person reunions. I plan an international flight.

My friend Rick suggests hypnotherapy as a way to access clues that may be buried in my subconscious. He did it once and was able to recall his early childhood memories from Japan with clarity. He tells me that it's more like re-experiencing than remembering. Intrigued, I ask around and get a referral for a therapist named Dr. McGraw, whose practice is right on St. Augustine Beach.

I arrive at Dr. McGrath's office just moments before my first session start time. We have only an hour, and I'm worried that I have shorted myself the valuable time needed to dig into those buried memories. Although I'm late, she's not yet waiting for me and there is no receptionist in the makeshift lobby, which is actually a small hallway between offices. I read the names of magazines lying on side tables, I study framed coastal art hung on the salmon-colored walls. Finally Dr. McGraw emerges from a small room on to my right. She hands me a clipboard. "Please, fill the forms and come in when you're ready."

I list personal information, medical history, insurance numbers. I knock on her door and she answers.

"Come in, come in," Dr. McGraw looks nothing like I expected. She is petite, just taller than me, with wild curly hair in shades of amber and gold. Her face is not young, but not yet old either, and it suggests some kindness and much patience. Her voice is lilted with the cadence of southern Ireland.

"Sit, please. Be comfortable."

I sit on the couch, uncertain, uncomfortable. I watch the pot of flowers at her chair. A box of tissues rests on the table beside my couch.

"Please, Raina. Can you tell me what you are looking for?"

So I begin. I explain to Dr. McGraw my history, the age I came to the US, and why I am seeking subconscious memories now. I speak as quickly as possible, wanting to reserve as much time as possible for the hypnosis. She nods patiently, scribbling notes.

"Ok then, Raina," she begins, "this is what we will do. I will walk you through some processes in your mind, sort of escorting you through your mind's tunnel. You must be patient—it may not work on the first try. But if it does, you should not expect to have vivid memories. It won't be like watching images on a TV screen. And what you remember might not be accurate. This was a very long time ago and, like you mentioned, some of your memories might have been created from stories you've heard or from your imagination.

"The details might not be completely accurate, but you will have feelings and sensations, and those will be true. Trust the feelings and sensations. Trust your memory and your mind. Do you have any questions?"

I do not.

"Then just relax now and listen to my voice. I will guide you."

She does. With the music of Dr. McGraw's soft brogue leading me, my mind travels through a green, flowering garden. I descend a mossy stone staircase, and arrive in a small, lonely room.

I can't tell the room's size, for I don't know if I am my right size. I sense I am very small, smaller than I can ever remember being. I am sitting on a dirt floor, the walls are white, and there seem to be no windows. Two other people are in the room, and I am certain one is a woman. I can't see her face, and yet I can somehow look directly into it and know it is my own. I feel the emotions radiating from this woman: Stillness. Resignation. Security without joy. Overwhelming sadness.

My body is still in the therapist's office, and although I can no longer feel my body, I know that it is weeping the tears of this woman who has my face. I am full of her sorrow, and I know it is a grief that will never end. I have never known devastation like this, and it is insufferable.

I hear Dr. McGraw's voice calling me back. I feel I will die from so much of this faceless woman's sorrow, and yet I can't bear to leave. But that gentle voice is calling me, it walks me back up the stone steps and back through the garden. I have no control; I cannot resist its pull.

I awaken in Dr. McGraw's office with great tears coursing down my cheeks. The session was successful—so much so that the force of my remembering surprises even Dr. McGraw. She speaks softly, and though I don't hear her words I know she is trying to calm me, trying to help me process what I have just experienced.

"Next time, we'll go through the same steps and you'll remember more. Each time you should be able to make more progress. You did very well today, Raina. You were ready."

I collect tissues from the box next to me, embarrassed at the mess I have become. I nod, mumble thanks, gather my belongings, and leave.

I never return.

Something in the emotions of that room, of my unknown mother's face, halts me. The intensity of her loss is more than I can take. I have become aware of a tremendous and terrible truth, and my heart is not ready for it.

I cancel my plans to travel to Korea, to appear on the Korean TV show, to visit my orphanage. In early 2012, as a final far-flung effort, I contact Korean Adoption Services to post my placement photo and personal information on their Korean website. I cast that one crumb into the universe, and then I chose to move forward.

Part 3
Reclamation

"In my experience, ghosts are made up only of the living, people you know are out there but are forever out of range."

~ Adam Johnson

Unforgotten

Omma's letter, May 4, 2014

March 1, 2013, was a very windy day. My sister came to my house with her children and grandchildren and asked me "If your daughter Soojung wanted to meet you, would you meet her?" I said, "Of course." I left my information at the facility and thought that one day she would come to me. During the last thirty-four years I never forgot her, even for one second. That's why I left my record at the facility.

At 8:00 p.m. on March 16, 2013, my niece Hyungjeong called me when I was on the subway. She said "Aunt, it seems we found Soojung." I instantly said, "Okay." I was not myself suddenly. I could not think about anything. I could not see anything.

After the weekend, Monday came. Hyungjeong called me again. Hyungjeong asked me many questions. I said, "Yes, correct. Yes, she is Soojung." That was all I said. I saw Soojung's photo on the Internet; she was looking for me. The photo was taken at the facility when we were separated. When I saw her photo, I felt as if my heart would burst. I began to tremble rapidly. My mind went back to thirty-four years ago. My other niece, Jeesoo, who lives in New York, asked me to send her my photo. On March 21, Soojung wanted to have a DNA test, as she was not sure of me. I had no doubt she was my daughter but had a test anyway. On March 26, Jeesoo called me and said, "She is your daughter!"

There was no news the next few days. I was waiting, and she seemed to be in a panic. I was in a panic too, and could not do anything and did not know what to do. I told my husband and children about this, and they were so happy. Then my daughter Soojung called me and sent a letter saying she was happily married with four children.

*****

Early Spring 2013

The universe conspires. At the same time I am placing my information on the Korean Adoption Services website, my Korean mother is enlisting the help of her nieces—my cousins—to broaden the search for her lost daughter. In short order, they find my name and image on the KAS website. It takes just that one webpage with that one photo, along with some impossibly good luck and great timing, to bring us all together.

Once the DNA test confirms that Jeesoo's aunt is indeed my Omma, I tell my children that they now have a Korean grandmother, or *halmeoni*. The kids have always known that I was adopted from Korea, but they were too young to really understand. The most enthusiastic response comes from my oldest daughter, Malia, who pronounces that it's "cool" and wants to travel to Korea.

Brett's response is similarly simple. I explain the maternity confirmation. I show him photos and letters from Jeesoo.

"Do you think we look alike?"

"Oh yeah, definitely. You look just like her."

For some reason I don't like this but can't understand why. Haven't I always longed for a mother's face to reflect my own? And yet, now that I have one the reality of it seems so preposterous that I can't bring myself to accept it. My inability to comprehend a family resemblance is visceral and unexpected.

"My God, I can't believe this is happening. I don't know how to respond. I don't know what to do."

"Yeah. Wow. It's crazy."

I thought I'd get a bigger response from Brett, but he is still the man I married thirteen years ago. I don't really believe he'd become complex, introspective, and articulate just because his wife is entering reunion with her birth family. I can't convey the vast, complicated response that I'm struggling through, and he can't understand it. This experience is mine alone.

I find that the barriers that segregate the two parts of myself—Raina and Soojung—begin to blur. The childish fantasy of a Korean family has stepped through time and dimension into my very real world.

I dream-walk through these days. Nothing makes sense anymore. I tell Brett, I tell Mom and Dad, I tell Kim, I tell the kids, I tell some my friends. I repeat this unbelievable story so maybe in the telling it will start to seem real. This does not work.

So many people cry when they hear this tale: My family lost me. They loved me. They never stopped looking for me. I see the emotion enter their faces as their eyes start to water. Women openly weep; grown men suffer sudden allergy attacks. I have no tears of my own though, for the storytelling is like recounting a long-forgotten fairytale.

Once upon a time, in a Korean kingdom far away, a mythical princess was born. She was locked in a magical castle called America, where an American family kept her safe from the dangers of becoming real.

In the light of day I have no tears. At night, though, when I have no one to pretend for, the sorrow seeps like ink into my heart. I hold my breath and squeeze my eyes, fighting hard until I can't fight anymore. Then my grief comes in great, gulping waves that break over me, that break me. I think there could be nothing harder than this— if there is, how could anyone ever survive?

I hide my grief in the night. I control it like a prisoner.

Late one night, Brett finds me like this: curled up like a child in our massive bed, already gone in a salty sea of tears. He doesn't know this is my nightly ritual. He can't see that I am adrift in pathological mourning. He has no way to comprehend the depth and magnitude of this ocean; he has only known the shore.

He does his best. He lies with me, wraps his arms around me, and strokes my hair. Even with him enveloping me, I am so utterly alone, pulled under by the riptide of my sadness.

*****

The myth of me, composed of mostly lies, started with Sungrowon orphanage in Seoul. It continued through Holt International and was perpetuated by my good but naïve American parents. The only remaining evidence of my three-year existence in Korea fits into two thin airmail envelopes and the fragmented memories of the lies my parents had accepted almost thirty years ago.

I leaf through the documents of my adoption file. Some papers are yellowing now, and the typewritten print indicates an era before word processing and personal computers.

These are the lies and fabricated facts that I piece together from those sources:

In December 1978, Park Soo Jung was abandoned in the street with her name and birthday pinned to her shirt. She was found by the Noryangjin police, categorized as an orphan with no parents, and brought to the Sungrowon orphanage. In June 1979, she became the property of Holt Children's Services, reassigned as orphan K79-1364, and promptly labeled "Adoptable." On America's Independence Day in 1979, she was given a family birth registration (the equivalent of a US social security number) with the falsified information that she had no mother or father. Child K79-1364 was liberated of all traces of her original identity and family, and officially converted to a paper orphan. On July 27, 1979, she became the property of Friends of Children of Vietnam (FCVN) who would then act as Holt's proxy for her placement in the United States.

In November 1979, FCVN referred child K79-1364 to a hopeful, loving couple in Louisville, Kentucky. With this referral, the couple received medical history, falsified orphan documents, and photos of a despondent, forlorn child.

I hold those referral photos in my hands.

Imagine the first image, a small 2.5 x 4 inch black and white print with grainy texture and rounded corners. A child stands alone in the center of the photo on the dirt ground next to a wooden bench swing. She wears a flowered dress, which she clutches in a dimpled hand. One sleeve is rolled up past her elbow, and the other is rolled down to her wrist. Her hair is cropped, and her bangs lay straight across her forehead. Her small mouth curves into a frown that pushes her heavy toddler cheeks down. But it's her eyes that capture you. They make you pause, hold the photo slightly closer, maybe not believe that a child so young can possess eyes so ancient and haunting. You can see her tired, two-year-old soul through those eyes.

Now you flip to the second photo, a head shot. The Peter Pan collar of her dress is slightly turned up, and her head turns slightly to the right. Her face possesses a gravity that is more compelling than it is lovely. Her narrow, full-lipped mouth frowns below her tiny, crusty nose. Again, her eyes draw you in. Now you can see the details of her black irises and hooded eyelids. In those eyes rests a sadness and resignation agonizingly unnatural for a child. These are the eyes of a refugee, of a survivor.

Years after that photo was taken, Mom will tell me, "It was those eyes that made me fall in love with you. As soon as I saw those pictures, I wanted to make you smile. I wanted to put happiness in those eyes."

Many more years after that, Omma will tell me, "It was those eyes that haunted me. For thirty-three years, I never stopped seeing those big, sad eyes."

I read through adoption documents from the late seventies:

FCVN formal correspondence, August 1979

"Please excuse this form letter, we would rather communicate personally, but feel that our staff time is more wisely used in processing more important work."

Tips on the Care and Adjustment of Vietnamese and Other Asian Children in the United States," published by the US Department of Health and distributed by Holt Children's Services, 1975

"Eventually your child will begin to question why he could not remain with his natural parents. We suggest you tell him that you do not know the specific details, but you are sure that his parents loved him and that the only way they were able to give him a good home was to be unselfish by placing the child's needs in front of their own desire to rear him to maturity."

Medical Information pamphlet, provided by Holt Adoption Program, Inc., April 1975

"One of the areas of which you need to be conscious is that your new child won't always be grateful for your efforts. This is also true of one's natural children, but somehow it seems your special efforts in turning to another country for a child, along with your financial sacrifice, should guarantee a special rapport and appreciation from your adopted child. It just can't always be that way! But the good times and the sense of your own

contribution and self-worth will carry you through, if you just maintain your momentum!"
<u>Information packet from Holt Adoption Program, Inc., October 1977</u>

"Adolescence… is the time he tries to figure out '<u>Who</u> am I?' Curiosity about his original parents or background may become stronger. Holt Adoption shares with the adoptive families everything that is known to us about the child."

These documents—adoption files, pamphlets, false memories—they are all I've had to piece together my history. Beneath the mountain of lies, however, remain glimmers of unforgotten truth which has somehow brought me these new, more reliable sources: my own Korean family. Myth gives way to reality as Omma's story slowly winds its way from Korea to Florida through a series of translated letters and text messages.

*****

Omma's first letter, April 4, 2013

Soojung, Soojung, Soojung…

For the last thirty-five years I've been keeping you in my mind and calling your name secretly. I've never forgotten about you, not even once, and I've always been wondering where you are and if you are doing well. Even though I sent you away in a wrong decision, when your feelings against me go away as time passes, then hopefully you might find me one day. Since I left all the information about me at Sungrowon, I waited and waited for you to reach me. If I could go back to that time, I would have never sent you away, even if we starved to death in the street. And I've been living for many years with these thoughts that I would happily lay down my life if I ever got to see your face once again.

Soojung! How could I ever forget your name, even in a dream?

Every year on February 15, I wished you were happy and cooked seaweed soup for you.

How could I ever ask your forgiveness for any reason?

All I can say to you is that I am truly sorry.

I don't know how to express to you how much I feel sorry.

I am looking forward to talking with you more when we see each other one day.

*****

Letter to Omma, April 2013

Dear Korean mom and Korean family –

Hello. This is a short story of the important things that have happened in my life.

I arrived in the US on January 27, 1980. I was adopted by a family in Kentucky. My parents already had one little girl that was adopted from Korea too. She is a year and a half older than me, and her name is Kim. I grew up in a small town called Shepherdsville, Kentucky. I was good in school and had some friends, but I never really felt like I fit in very well. There were no other Asian kids, and sometimes the other kids made fun of me because I was adopted and I looked different than they did. In high school, I played soccer and tennis, but I wasn't very good at either one.

I went to college at West Point, New York, in 1994. West Point is the big military academy for the US Army. I had to study a lot and exercise a lot, and when I graduated I was commissioned as an officer in the US Army. When I was a senior in college, I met the man whom I was going to marry. His name is Brett, and he also graduated from West Point. After graduation we were both army officers. We got married in 2000.

My first job in the Army was an engineer, and I was stationed in Camp LaGuardia, Korea. That is in Uijeongbu. I went to Seoul a lot, mainly Yongsan, and some areas around there. I also went to Dongducheon, where Camp Casey is. So I lived in Korea for a whole year, and I never knew that my Korean family was there.

When I came back to the US from Korea, I lived in Texas. I got pregnant and had a little girl. She was born in 2002. We named her Malia. That was the same time that 9/11 happened in the US, so we were also doing a lot of army training and preparing to fight in the wars in Iraq and Afghanistan. It was such a busy time! When I had my little girl I wondered what my Korean family would think about her, and whether she looked like anyone in my Korean family.

My husband went to Iraq to fight in the war in 2004. I was pregnant again, so I stayed in Texas and had a little boy in 2004. His name is Ty. Then Brett came home from Iraq, and we both got out of the Army in 2005. We moved to Tennessee. Then his job made us move to St. Augustine, Florida in 2006. I also got pregnant again, and in 2006, I had a son named Cade. So we had three kids: Malia, Ty, and Cade.

In 2009, we adopted a daughter from China. She was six-and-a-half years old when we adopted her. Her birthday is in 2003, and her name is Maia. So now we have four kids: Malia, Maia, Ty, and Cade.

In 2010, my husband Brett lost his job because the US economy was so bad. He decided to work in Afghanistan for a year and a half. He worked there and then came home. Now Brett stays home with the kids and coaches them in all their different sports. Malia plays soccer, Maia plays lacrosse, Ty plays baseball, and Cade plays baseball and football. I work at a big company that makes airplanes. I am very busy with work, and I am in charge of a group of people who work very hard. I am also in graduate school, studying to earn my MBA. I'm quite busy!

Now I will explain some things about how I have felt in my life and some interesting things about me, so you can feel more like you know me.

When I was first adopted, I had a lot of trouble adjusting to my new family. I cried a lot and had nightmares. I was scared of being taken away. I slowly learned to trust my new family. They have always loved me very much and always took really good care of me and my sister. I have lots of American cousins and aunts and uncles. But most of my life I did not feel like I fit in. My personality was so different from them. I felt sad a lot. I thought I had memories of Korea, but I didn't know if they were really memories or just dreams. I thought I remembered my Korean mother, but I didn't think that could be true.

Most of my life, most people have considered me very smart. I think fast and can do harder work than a lot of people. I'm grateful to have a good mind and a loving family.

When I moved to Korea while I was in the Army, I felt very scared of going to Korea. I thought Korea was a sad and empty place for me. When I arrived, I found out it was a beautiful place, and I had so much fun there. I loved the food and the people. But I did not fit in.

When we adopted our daughter from China, I started to learn more about adoption from Korea and China. I learned that the adoptions in Korea in the seventies and eighties were usually unethical. It made me feel sad and angry that Korea would separate so many families. Since I had kids, I felt that no mother would ever want to be separated from her children and that my own mother must be terribly sad that I was taken away from her. I started to wonder where my Korean family was, and if they remembered me and ever thought about me too. I thought that my Korean mother must miss me very much and must have tried so hard to keep me. In January 2012, I decided to contact Holt and KCARE to tell them to put my information on their websites. I did not think that my Korean family would ever find me though.

So when you contacted me, I felt surprised. I feel happy and sad. I have had a wonderful life, and I have a wonderful family, but now I realize that I could have had a wonderful Korean life and family too, if things had been different. I don't feel anything bad toward anyone in my Korean family. Now, I mostly feel lucky that I have an American family who loves me so much they have given me a wonderful life, and a Korean family who loved me enough to never give up hope of finding me. I wish I could have both lives with both families, my American life and my Korean life, but time has gone by, and we can only have the future.

*****

Letter from brother, Hyunsik, April 5, 2013

엄마랑닮았냐고물어본거같아.
I think you asked me if I look alike with my mom.

엄마닮았으면좀더똑똑하고머리도작았을걸??
별로안닮은거같아ㅎㅎ눈에쌍커플정도만닮았음.
If I was I should be smarter and my head should be smaller too. so I don't think I am, lol. maybe just eyelids.

너가엄마닮아서머리가좋은걸거야..
엄마식구들이다똑똑해(이모애들처럼,   지수등등)
.키같은건안닮은게다행이지ㅎㅎ

*I think you are more like my mother side.. Her side
families are smart (like my cousons, Jeesoo etc.) you're
lucky that you're not like my mother in hights. Lol*

그리고난아빠를많이닮았어.
and i'm more alike with my father.

사실아버지가다른거에대해서좀충격이였지.
그래도엄마딸이니까..
*actually my father was shocked by something else but
still you are her kid..*

어렸을때부터누나있는친구들이부러웠었거든..
I've been always envy those kids that has a sister..

누나들이동생들많이챙겨주고잘해주니까.
Since sisters usually takes care of their little brother.

머지금은다컸지만..
Well~ I'm all grown up now

그래도아빠도딸한명더생겼다고좋아하시고머나
도누나생겨서좋긴해.
*Anyway my father loves about that he can have a
daughter and so I do.*

미국이라는나라가말로만많이들었지나한테크게
의미가있는나라는아니였어..
*Until now, USA didn't mean anything to me but just a
word you listen often.*

어렸을때이사실을알았다면영어공부를열심히했
겠지..했을가?? 그래도안했을거같기도하고..

I must study harder if I knew about all this...maybe?
maybe not..

내가돈을많이벌면엄마도미국도종종보내드리고
우리가족도같이가고했을텐데..

I wish I earn more money so I can send my mother to
US occasionally and also all my family..

사실현재상황으로는벅차긴해.
한달벌어서한달사는정도..
나의아빠도엄마미국보내드린다고돈열심히모으고있
어ㅎㅎ

well right now it's kind of tough. just living like month
to month.. My father is also saving his money to send her
to US lol

엄마한테보낸편지는나도봤어.
그날엄마가좀슬퍼하는거같더라..의정부에있었다면차
로한시간거리였는데 .. 많이아쉽다..

I have read your letter to her. She looked quite sad all
day.. If you were in Uijeongbu, it was just a distance for
an hour with car.. that's a shame..

입양,가족찾기머이런말들이나랑아무상관없는말
인줄알고살았었지.
티비드라마에서나나오는일이라고..

Adoption, finding missing family.. I've never had any
thought about any of these. It's just things in TV drama..

근데그런일이나한테일어날줄이야상상도못했어.
never imagined it could happen to me

자꾸메일도보내고하는것도가족이니까서로알아
가야되지않겠나. 하는나의작은노력이야.

*keep emailing you is just to know each other more
since we are family.. a little effort of me.*

사는곳이멀어서보지는못하지만.
그게말이틀려서좀어려울뿐이지.

*can't visit to see you because of a distance but I think
It's just little harder because of language.*

그러면서나도정리가되는거같고...
요몇주내가일이잘안되고좀멍해있거든..

*and I guess I cleared up my head too... things didn't
work out well for me so I was kind of dazed for past
couple weeks..*

지금누나의삶에우리가도와준건하나도없지만그
래도공부도잘하고애들도넷이나키우고참대단한거같
어.

*I'm really happy that you are rasing four kids and
studied well. it is great and i'm proud of you even we
couldn't support you anything.*

그만큼많은노력이있었겠지.
내가살았었던시간하고비교해보면많이힘들었을거라
생각해.

*you've must been putting a lot of efforts through your
life, I think you probably had hard time compared to mine.*

서로닮진않았어도사는곳도틀려도생활이틀려도
볼순없어도그래도누나라고생각하며살고있을게.
원하는모든것들이잘되기를바랄게.

*Even though we are not look alike, living in different
countries, life styles and we can't see each other, I think*

you are my sister.
    and wish your best on everything you do

*****

Letter from Omma, April 7, 2013

수정아내가이이름을이렇게자주부를수있을줄은
한번도생각하지못했는데이젠너의이름만생각해도행
복하구나. 지난번너의글을보고너무나미안한마음에두
서없는글을보냈구나. 아직은내가엄마라는지칭을쓸수
가없구나. 엄마가아닌그냥나라는사람의글을봐주길바
란다.
아직도내머리속의마음속의수정이는눈망울이맑고큰,
네가간직한성로원에서준작은아기,
그아기가내딸이란다.
그런데현재의너의모습과너의행복한가족사진을보면
너무나멀리와있는것같구나.
그래도너무나예쁘게잘자란너의모습과사랑스런아이
들, 예쁘고똑똑해보이는할리아,   밝고명랑한나이아,
씩씩하고잘생긴카이,   장난스럽게생긴귀여운엘비,
믿음직하고잘생긴브렛을보면서너무나행복한가족을
느끼고있단다.

Dear Soojung,

*I never thought I could call your name so often like I
do these days. It makes me so happy every time just
thinking about it. I'm sorry for the rambling, emotional
letter that I wrote after reading yours last time. Maybe I
am not ready to call myself your mother yet. I hope you
read my letter just as coming from a person, not from a
mother.*

My daughter that I remember is still a baby girl with beautiful, big eyes, just like the girl in that picture you have from Sungrowon. When I look at the pictures of you and your happy family, I realize that it took a long time to find each other. But I also can see my pretty and well-grown girl and her lovely children—pretty and smart-looking Malia, bright and cheerful-looking Maia, handsome and brave-looking Ty, playful and cute Cade— and reliable and handsome Brett making a very happy family in that picture. I am so proud of you and thankful for your courage and wisdom, and for being so well throughout your life.

The Gift of Seaweed Soup

Omma's letter, May 4, 2014

After I received the letter, I cried continually at the empty house and regretted my wrong decision. I sent her photos of myself and my family. One month passed, and I decided to visit the USA. On my birthday, my son gave me a flight ticket, and my husband and daughter told me that they would pay my expenses to visit the USA. I felt like I was dreaming. I could not believe what was happening. It was too long to wait until October. I felt uneasy every day, waiting and waiting. I tried to go back to normal life, but it was so hard.

On May 14, Jeesoo called me. She said that Soojung would come to Korea on May 29. I couldn't say anything. The day was so long. I wondered what I would say to her when I saw her, what I should tell her, what I would eat with her…I remembered my past… On March 17, 1956, in a poor Korean village after the Korean War…

At 8:50 pm on May 29, 2013, I went to Incheon airport with my son. My sister, Hyunjeong, my younger sister, and her husband all came to the airport. I felt that the waiting time was too long. Finally, thirty-seven-year-old Soojung went from being in a photo to coming out in real life. When I saw Soojung, I felt so sorry for her and was afraid of seeing her. I could not look into her eyes. I brought her to my home and introduced my family and let her rest, as she seemed tired from the jetlag. The next morning, I made seaweed soup for Soojung. I spent the whole day with her but still could not believe it. During the last thirty-four years, I imagined a little three-year-old daughter, but she was now taller than I and had a new name, so I was confused.

*****

Late Spring 2013

I spend the morning in a frenzy. Just two weeks ago I made the impromptu decision to travel to Korea to meet Omma, and there is still so much to do before my flight tonight.

Yesterday I bought a new suitcase at the last minute—an enormous monstrosity specially selected for this trip. My old suitcase was thirteen years old, bought just before my first adult trip to Seoul. It had traveled across the Pacific when I was still in the dark, when I was still terrified of both my past and my future. Today the zipper is busted, a foot has broken off, and it uses half of my allowable weight even when empty.

My new suit case is a symbol of the future. It's silver in color like the jet that will carry us, light, and sleek with modern amenities like 360-degree wheels and expandable capacity. When I dragged it into the house, Brett and I laughed together at its ridiculous enormity. This luggage is my ark; I am ready for the flood.

I leave for the airport in a few hours, and my procrastination punishes me. I throw a week's worth of clothing and sundries into my cavernous new suitcase. I add the wrapped gifts I have selected for the people I know about: Disney World T-shirts for the nieces and nephews, vitamins for the adults, and candies for anyone else. Even with all this, my mule of a suitcase is still only half-full. The fact of its emptiness seems appropriate, for this is how I make my transitions. As a toddler coming to the US, as a teenager leaving for West Point, as a young lieutenant returning to Korea, I've done with little but myself.

My bags are ready, which leaves one last task: I climb a rolling ladder to the top of our wall of bookcases—my favorite feature of our home—where the old family photo albums reside. I flip through the yellowed sticky pages, peeling clear plastic sheets away from vintage family photos. I use my iPhone to snap digital copies of actual pictures: our first family photo at O'Hare International, me dressed as a curly-haired witch on Halloween, Dad building us a snowman.

My plan is to compile them into an album of my life while on a brief stopover in Los Angeles. This is my gift for my Korean mother, a gesture to give her back just a little of all those years she lost. Brett watches me scurrying around, loading my iPhone with old photos. He jokes that the photos won't give her back anything, they'll just rub the loss in her face. *Look at how wonderful the years were without you. Look at what you missed.* Then he decides that the gift album is a good preemptive strike to make them cry first because the best defense is a good offense.

His jokes make me laugh, but they ring a bit true. What if my gift is hurtful? What if she is sensitive and sentimental, and I drive her into despair? But I am her daughter, and I sense that I am like her in many ways. She won't sink into sorrow. She is strong and grateful—like me, she has already begun to move forward and heal.

I hug the kids. I forget to eat. I leave.

Thirty-three years ago, a United Airlines flight took me away from my first family and country. Today, another United Airlines flight reverses that path.

On the first leg of the flight, Jacksonville to Denver, I read Jane Jeong Trenka's *The Language of Blood.* Her book speaks to me; some parts are so close to my experience that I could have (or wish I had) written them. Other parts are uniquely hers. The memoir resonates as truth, and I decide that is both an awful and a perfect selection to start this voyage.

After a short visit with friends in Los Angeles, I embark on the real purpose of this trip. I board an afternoon flight from LAX where, after a couple of layovers, I'll meet a new Korean family at Incheon International. They will claim they are mine and I am theirs, and we have the DNA to prove it.

Right away the trip begins badly, with my LAX flight delayed several hours. By the time that first leg touches down in San Francisco, I'm distraught. I'm already scheduled for the last night flight into Incheon, and if I don't get back on track, I'll lose a day in Korea. I race off the plane to learn I have missed the connecting flight.

Somehow, miraculously, the airline attendant books me on the very next flight to Narita where I'll be able to catch the original flight that takes me to Incheon. I'm back on track.

I force myself to stay awake on the longest leg of the flight from SFO to Narita, knowing I have a late-evening arrival in Korea. I want to be tired when I get there. I fill the time watching two American movies and two Korean movies. The Korean movie is about a mentally disabled man that gets mistakenly convicted of murdering a little girl, leaving his own daughter alone in the world. She sneaks into the prison to live with him and his wonky cellmates. When he is executed, I weep.

I eat a little of the airplane food, but not too much because I want to be hungry when I arrive in Korea too. My layover in Japan is uneventful, and the final flight is about two and a half hours from Narita to Incheon. I nap.

The pilot announces our preparation for arrival and I wake, expecting to feel some anticipation but still feeling none. I'm in an emotionless form of survival mode.

I watch the lights of Seoul glide by below. They are the lights of ten million *hanguk* Korean people, in the most densely populated city in the world, people who consume the most hard liquor per capita in the world. *What are your huddled masses numbing themselves from? Why so much national shame? What secrets do you hold, and what future can you possibly offer?*

We arrive at the gate, and I gather my belongings. I make a quick stop at the ladies room to brush my teeth and check my hair—first impressions are important. At the baggage carousel, I learn that although I have made it to Korea as scheduled, my mule of a suitcase, my dear companion and ark, is delayed in San Francisco. I'll have to make my entry alone.

I emerge from exit D of the international terminal and scan the many Korean faces huddled in the waiting area—so many! This place seems so foreign and yet so familiar. I hear my name—Raina!—and see a waving arm. My vision zooms in to three tiny *ajumma* who look just like the photos I have been studying the last two months. I move toward them, and one moves toward me.

This woman is tiny. She looks so much like the face I've seen in pictures and strangely like the one I've seen in the mirror. My mind still has trouble with this idea, that I should bear a family resemblance. *Omma*. Mother. Mom. I practice associating the words with her face.

She tries to wrap her arms around me, but already she is weakened from a lifetime of guilt and grief, and she loses her strength. She cannot stand. Others in our group catch her, I don't know who they are. She is half-collapsed, half-carried to a bench, but she keeps her arms wrapped around me. She's not letting go for anything, never letting her baby go again.

There's a terrible pressure growing in my chest, but I retain my composure. I have wondered my whole life what this moment would feel like—to look into my own Omma's face, to be wrapped in her arms. Now I know: in this moment, although I have the emotions inside, I am as controlled as always. It's the same as when I first met each of my children, the same as when I met Maia—but this time there is no one around for me to mimic. There is no right way, for this moment is unprecedented.

I distract myself from the gravity of the moment by inventorying the others in our group. There is a beautiful, petite young woman who mumbles bits of English to me: *hello Soojung, get imo a tissue, this is your aunt, this is your brother*. She is my cousin Hyunjung, Jeesoo's sister. There is an astoundingly large man with a slack, expressionless face—this is Omma's first son, my younger half brother Hyunsik. Nearby there are two women whom I immediately recognize as Omma's sisters, and one of them is with her husband. They are also crying.

For a while we stand there like that: Omma weeping and holding me, Hyunjung taking care of business, aunts sobbing, Hyunsik waiting, me feeling astounded. After a short time, I am gently pushed to leave. The younger imo and her husband say goodbye. The rest of us—Omma, little brother, younger cousin, older imo and myself—load into a white car and head toward Omma's home in Hwaseong. I sit in the backseat with Omma, her arms still wrapped around me.

*****

This part of my journey requires a new vocabulary.

There are words whose English equivalents I speak, but whose true meaning I struggle to understand:

엄마, *omma,* mother

이모, *imo,* aunt, mother's sister

이모부, *imobu,* uncle, mother's sister's husband

삼촌, *samchon,* uncle, mother's brother

언니, *unni*, older sister

남동생, *namdongsaeng*, younger brother

여동생, *dongsaeng* younger sister

할머니, *halmeoni*, grandmother

할아버지, *harabeoji*, grandfather

가족, *gajok*, family

There are words with no English equivalents whose meaning I understand but had no way to express:

한, *han*, an intrinsic Korean emotion of sorrow, grief, oppression, isolation, loneliness, and resentment of suffering which leads to forgiveness and deep love. As described by President Josiah Bartlett in season five of *The West Wing:* "There is no literal English translation [for han]. It's a state of mind. Of soul, really. A sadness. A sadness so deep no tears will come. And yet still there's hope."

정, *jeong*, a culturally specific type of Korean love, borne of empathy, compassion, pathos, and emotional attachment. As described by Jane Jeong Trenka in *Fugitive Visions:* "[Jeong is] that emotion unknown by individualist Western cultures, that emotion that makes Koreans say not 'Korea,' 'Korean language,' or 'my mother' – but 'our country,' 'our language,' and 'our mother.'"

*****

It's morning. My mind climbs out of slumber, and the slow remembering begins. This is Korea. I have been sleeping in my Omma's bed. I am not still dreaming.

Omma and Older Imo are in the kitchen doing what they do best, and breakfast is already prepared. Hyunjung is at the ready as our translator. Breakfast is miyeokguk, seaweed soup, which Koreans traditionally serve as a birthday meal. Omma tells me how she has prepared this soup for me every birthday and cried my name in despair, *Soojung-ah! Soojung-ah!* But today she serves this gift of seaweed soup with joy, for it is like a birthday celebration: a rebirth of our family ties which were torn apart so long ago. Omma ladles my serving of miyeokguk over rice as I sample the various banchan: cabbage kimchi, cucumber kimchi, others that I don't recognize.

Omma has an extensive menu planned—she is making up for a lifetime of missed meals. She serves me her tenderness and sorrow, bite by bite, and dish by dish. She loves me as all mothers love their children: by feeding them.

Omma's husband joins us for breakfast. I am his wife's illegitimate child from another man, her surprise American daughter, so I'm not sure what he will think of me. From time to time I notice he is watching me, and I quickly realize there is no hostility in his gaze. Midway through the meal, he pushes more food in my direction and smiles.

"*Meogeo! Meogeo!* Eat! Eat!"

These are universal words of truce and nurturing, so I understand we are friends. I call him *Appa*, father.

Eunjin is my sister, the youngest of Omma's children. She is tall, like her father and her brother, with broad features and a quick, easy grin. Her face does not hold anything back; it is the face of a woman who has known love, acceptance, and security her whole life.

Eunjin arrives with her son, Jooeun, and greets me with a breathless flourish. She and Appa both leave for work, leaving Omma, Imo, Hyunjung and myself to talk. Hyunjung is embarrassed about her level of English proficiency, but she is a fantastic translator. Omma and Imo laugh about palli; they tell me the spirit of palli is what built this country. They reminisce about their poor lives and how much is different today. We sip scalding, sugary instant coffee from tiny paper cups in the usual Korean fashion, and from time to time these two sisters who have been through so much together wear the same nostalgic sadness in their eyes. They have seen so much in their lifetimes.

Omma wants me to walk with her. We step outside her apartment and find our sandals in the family of shoes that lives outside her door. We ride the elevator down twelve floors and step outside into the hazy morning sunshine.

On our walking path, Omma holds my hand. She seems to never want to let me go, and although I have never been comfortable with physical affection, I'm glad for this gesture. Maybe it's wrong, maybe I am selfish, but I take comfort in knowing that losing me hurt.

There is a small patch of vegetables along the edge of our path, and Omma walks over to it. She points at a section about twelve feet long, then points at herself. She gets down on her knees and pretends to plant seeds and harvest onions, lettuce, and eggplants. I understand, this is her plot. From this soil, commingled with her sweat and devotion, Omma cultivates sustenance for her family.

She points and gives me the words: *sangchu* lettuce, *pa* onion, *mu* radish. I watch the gentle way she handles her small crop, and I try to imagine her life. It's a life dedicated to providing for others—her husband, children, and grandchildren. It's a life that has had so much taken from it, and has demanded little in return. As Omma teaches me her vocabulary of nourishment, I see God in all the small things of her garden. Omma might believe that her life has been insignificant, but from it she has done His work quietly and steadily, despite so many reasons she could have turned inward. In this moment I see the greatness of this tiny, tough woman, and I vow to not fail her legacy.

We return to the house and talk more. Hyunsik and Hyunjung have taken some time off work, and we fill the days getting to know each other. At the East China Sea there is a sailing festival where we walk along the vendor booths. Brother gets bored, so we go bowling. We play on teams, first me and Hyunjung face off with Imo and Hyunsik. Then we realign teams, and it is Hyunsik with me against Imo and Hyunjung. I am terrible, but we laugh and cheer each other on.

*****

I am alone with Omma and Imo. Hyunjung has left us for a short while, so we have no translator, which leaves Omma and Imo to continue their never-ending sisterly chatter and me to spectate. There is a particular moment when Omma and Imo appear to have made a decision, and Omma stands.

Omma leaves the main room where we spend most of our time, the one in the center of her apartment. I don't know which of the bedrooms she has left to, but moments later she returns carrying a large, flat box in both hands. It is the size of a medium Amazon shipping parcel and light for its size.

She beckons me to her. As I approach, Omma lifts the lid from the box, revealing the brilliant garments within. It is her *hanbok*.

Hanbok is Korea's traditional dress. The rich history of its silks, the deep symbolism of its cut, these mesmerized me from the first I learned about it while living in Korea thirteen years earlier. As you consider *cheongsam* with China, *kimono* with Japan, and *ao dai* with Vietnam, you should consider hanbok with Korea. It dates back over sixteen hundred years from the Chosun dynasty, and each element of hanbok holds its own symbolic meaning—everything from the curve of the neck and wrist lines to the colors and patterns of the fabric. In modern Korea, hanbok is reserved for special occasions like weddings or formal events. It is the cultural clothing of my mother and her country, it is the embodiment of

Korean history, and to me it is the most beautiful and distinct of all traditional attire.

Omma lifts the garments from the box, whites and pinks floating in her hands like great clouds of cotton candy and love. She sorts out a white, slip-like garment and holds it toward me. I realize she means for me to put it on. In a moment that feels like an unexpected dream, I carry the slip to her bedroom, remove my tired American clothes, and slide the slip over my head. This is the first layer, the *sokchima*. I step back into the main room where Omma and Imo wait.

Next, Omma lifts a massive, flowing sheet of dark pink silk and holds it up at arm's length. She stands before me, gestures for me to lift my arms, and then from my front, she slides the thin white straps to my shoulders to allow the pink shirt to hang from my armpits to the floor. This is the *chima*, or skirt, and it is soft and billowy like music. I notice an exquisite white embroidery detail along the bottom half of the chima. Omma smooths the flowing skirts all around me, then reaches behind me to pull the chima straps back to my front and ties them at the top of my chest. She fusses over the small bow, making sure it is even and flat.

This is enough, I think. Just this one long, elegant garment has fulfilled every transformative wish I've ever had, but Omma is not finished.

Next she grasps an almost sheer white jacket with dark blue ribbons streaming from its front. As she holds it up, I see that the jacket is also silk and trimmed in small pink embroidery flowers. Again I hold out my arms as Omma pulls the long sleeves over them and then ties it closed. I feel centuries of heritage in this short, simple jacket, this *jeogori* that my ancestors once wore.

"*Otgoreum*," she tells me, holding forth the blue silk ribbons in her hand. They are so long they puddle in the floor around my skirts. Omma lifts and manipulates them into a large, single-looped bow and steps back.

With a disapproving look, Omma steps forward.

"Tut, tut," she clicks her tongue, unravels the ribbon, and works it again. This bow looks the same as the first to me, but Omma is now satisfied.

She finally hands me two tiny white socks with a strange seam running down the top and pointy, silken shoes. I pull them onto my feet and then clutch a tiny silk purse. The transformation is complete.

I make my way to a mirror, and for a second I see with an eight-year-old's eye. I see once upon a time and a kingdom far, far away where a Korean princess lived in a lonely tower. I've become the dream I once had.

Then Omma stands next to me and I see something even more miraculous—I see my mother's daughter. Omma's face shines with unabashed pride to be living in this moment neither of us thought possible. Together, we have stepped through the looking glass, and the White Queen tells us this memory of an alternate future.

*****

That night of my first full day with my Korean family, we sit to a dinner fit for royalty. Omma and Imo prepare *dakbokkeumtang*, a spicy chicken stew, because I said I loved the similar *daktoritang* while I was stationed in Uijeongbu. Hyunjung and I watch iPhone videos of my kids and exchange Korean and English language lessons. Eunjin and Appa return from work, and Appa sets to work bringing out the portable grill and *bulgogi*, marinated beef, to the balcony. He sets up a low bapsang dinner table and we all sit on the balcony floor around it. Omma jokes that we are "eating out." Omma, Imo, and Hyunsik all have persistent dry humor—always joking, always laughing at others' jokes. Appa grills the bulgogi, and Hyunsik's wife joins us for dinner. I have a can of Hite beer, and Appa has a bottle of soju. The house is so full of people and food. My heart is so full of love for a family I've just met. My belly is just plain full.

With Hyunjung as our translator, Appa interviews me about my time at West Point and in the Army. Wasn't it hard for me? Wasn't the training difficult? Since reading the letter I sent, he has worried about that—such a small girl doing such hard tasks. We discuss what the Military Academy was like, how it was for me to be small and train in the Army. We compare my military experience with my brother's. Hyunsik is more than a foot taller than me and probably three times my weight, and because of his large stature, he was stationed at the DMZ. But Appa jokes that Hyunsik was a weakling who complained, and that his new daughter is the strongest.

After dinner we pack up small bags to spend a night at Hyunjung's apartment in Seoul. I don't have much to pack since my suitcase still has not arrived. I've been wearing the same clothes for over two days, but I'm finding that I don't really need much else of what I packed. What I need to sustain me, at least for a little while, is already here.

Appa argues with Hyunjung—why do we have to leave? He wants to spend more time with me. He wants to understand me better, get to know more about my life and my experiences. I am grateful for his acceptance.

On the drive to Seoul, I am astonished by the way this family converses with each other. They are so easy together. They have such affection, which shows in how they do not fight, how they joke at each other's expense. *She is the prettier sister. He is lazy and not smart.* These little insults are their culture of endearment. Along the drive, Omma clutches my hands and expresses her grief and guilt. My cousin's translation is simple, but I understand with my heart.

A Ghost of Sangju

Omma's letter, May 4, 2014

> *On May 31, we went Seoul and went to a traditional Korean clothing shop and measured her size. We ate cold noodles and went to Myeongdong and Insadong, and we saw many things together. The next day, we went my hometown, Sangju. We bowed at my parents' graves. I would not regret the past; as I bowed to my father's grave, I swore it. We met my elder brother and nephews and had a good time together.*

*****

I wake earlier than everyone but do not get up. We are at Hyunjung's apartment in Seoul. All the women—Omma, Imo, Hyunjung, myself—have slept on blankets spread over the floor, and we take up the entire main room. Hyunsik,the lone man in our funny little troupe, sleeps alone in Hyunjung's bedroom.

Early in the morning, my suitcase finally arrives. I rummage through its contents: clean clothes, my familiar toothbrush, a change of shoes. Most importantly, I can finally deliver the gifts that I meant to present when I arrived—they were to be my peace offerings. Omma and Imo immediately pore over the photo album. They study my face through the years; they watch me grow in the pages before their eyes. In Omma's heart I have still been baby Soojung, wearing my white hat and crying for her. I think that through the images of this photo album, she can finally let go of that child and realize the woman I am now.

Hyunjung leaves for work, briefly leaving me without a translator until her sister arrives. The rest of us eat a huge delicious breakfast—*soondubu*, spicy tofu soup;

gelatinous *mulbammuk* and *dotorimuk*; yams; boiled eggs; and kimchi.

Hyunjung's oldest sister, Young, arrives. She is a flounce of yellow coat and brassy orange hair. Young possesses an electric energy and confidence, and her presence takes up twice her physical space. She is a juxtaposition of elegance and unpretentiousness. Young works as an English teacher, and now that she's here I have a voice again. Young has brought her youngest daughter, a playful toddler who is not willing to call me imo.

The whole group of us head out for *patbingsu*—a concoction of shaved ice, sweet red beans, and ice cream—before a day of shopping in Dongdaemun. We fill up on the icy sweetness, coffee bingsu is my favorite. Then Young leaves us to head for work, and we take the train to Dongdaemun. Omma, Imo, and Hyunsik have been my constant companions, and we have grown comfortable with each other.

I have dreamed of owning a hanbok since I lived in Korea thirteen years ago, so I ask and Omma does not deny me. I select a great, full crimson skirt with a tidy white jacket and navy blue sash. These colors are appropriate for my marital status, colors that represent the flags of both of my countries, America and Korea.

Jeesoo has arranged for a friend to meet us at the hanbok vendor so we can communicate better than Hyunjung's limited fluency allows. Her name is Soojung like mine, but she assumes the name of Chris when speaking English. Though she is native Korean, Chris's English is fluent with no accent at all. She is startlingly beautiful with razor cheekbones a mile high and waist-length hair like sheets of spun black silk. She has a comfortable, breezy demeanor. Seoul is her city, and we are her guests.

We leave the hanbok vendor in Dongdaemun and ride

the subway to Myeongdeong, where I can shop for souvenirs. On the way, we have lunch at a naengmyeon restaurant where we slurp chewy buckwheat noodles from an icy cold, spicy broth. I can't seem to get enough of this country's culinary bounty.

With Chris as our translator, Omma has the freedom to speak freely without fear of mistranslation. She asks Hyunsik to leave. It's his birthday, and I feel sorry that I've taken the attention away from him, but for Omma today is only about me. Hyunsik is a good man, this new little brother of mine, and he cheerfully leaves us to our private conversation. How turbulent this must be for him—to be displaced as the oldest son, to discover such scandalous secrets in his own family. I love him already for his quiet, quirky humor, for his patience with all of us batty women, for his stumbling attempts to speak English, and mostly for his sincere willingness to accept an unknown American sister.

*****

Omma is like a deep and mighty river that has been dammed for too long. The reservoir of her sorrow seeps out one story at a time. She begins slowly at first, rocking herself a bit and catching the shining beads that fall from the corners of her eyes. Chris listens patiently and nods sympathetically as Omma's stories grow longer and her tears fall heavier. Although we are in a full public restaurant, we are entirely alone in the intensity of our conversation. Through Chris's translation, this is the story I hear:

"Oh, Soojung-ah! I was a stupid, stupid girl. Such a weak and stupid girl. Everything is my fault. How can I ever ask your forgiveness? I'm so sorry for everything; it's all my fault.

"I was young and became pregnant and I had

nowhere to go. We were homeless, Soojung, we had nothing. We lived on the street, and I thought we'd die there. Your father died like that! He just died of alcoholism in the street! I tried to find work, but how could I work? I asked my sister to take you in so I could find work, and she did.

"My sister's husband loved you very much. Whenever he left the house, you tried to follow him. Since you weren't registered, you didn't have a family name. He loved you so much he wanted to register you in his family name, to raise you as his daughter. But then he was betrayed by a friend on a loan, and they lost everything. They were almost homeless now too! They couldn't care for you anymore, so I took you back.

"You are Soojung—it means crystal. I gave you the name because I wanted you to be pure. You didn't have a lot of hair, so I always took you out in a white hat. I should have bought a new white hat for you now. You had such large eyes, such beautiful eyes, and everyone always commented on your large eyes. You were a good baby. You never cried except when I weaned you.

"I carried you on my back to look for a job. I took you back to Sangju where I lived as a girl, and where my father and my brother still lived. No one would help us; they wanted to but their wives, my stepmother and my sister-in-law, said no. Nobody helped me. I thought we would die in the streets together like your father.

"Then I heard about Sungrowon, and I thought they could take care of you so I could find a job. I thought it was temporary; I'd find work and then get you back, but they told me I had to go to Noryangjin police station and sign some papers. So you could eat and be safe, I signed the papers. I was a weak and stupid girl.

"I visited you every day, and at first that was okay. But then after a while they told me to stop visiting you, that it made you cry when I left, and that you were being sent for adoption. I panicked then, and I went to my sister and told them what happened, that Sungrowon was sending you away. They didn't know any of this. They thought we were doing well, but when they heard about Sungrowon they went straight over and demanded to take you back.

"Sungrowon refused. They said the only way to get you back was to pay the adoption fees that they had already received to send you away. So your uncle left, and they saved up the money—it was so much money!—and they were happy. They even bought you a new outfit, and they took the money and the outfit but Sungrowon had already sent you away. They refused to tell us anything after that.

"My husband started chasing me soon after that. I told him all these terrible things and I tried to make him leave me alone, but he loved me and accepted me anyway. But I was never a good mother after that. I couldn't give my other children good love. Always when Eunjin tried to hug me, I pushed her away. She would cry and I still pushed her away.

"Ten years ago I went to Sungrowon. I left my information and gave them the only pictures I had of us together, and when I didn't hear from them/you, I thought you didn't want to know me. Then your uncle died of cancer. Imo and I got scared that we'd die too without ever finding you. So we asked Jeesoo and Hyunjung to help.

"When Jeesoo sent me the picture they found of Park Soojung on the website, I knew it was my own baby Soojung. I can't forget my baby's big eyes. I never forgot the look in my child's eyes at Sungrowon. I knew we found you."

Our conversation goes on for only an hour—so much to say in so little time. We become heavy from it. I ask about my father a few times, but Omma evades the topic.

She only says that he was older, that he was smart like me, and that he died. She didn't know, or wouldn't tell, anymore about him than that. I won't find out the full truth of her youth and my father until a year later.

*****

If you drive from Seoul to Sangju, you travel back in time. The road emerges from the dense city through vertical skyscraper suburbs, where the vast Korean population huddles in the country's narrow corridors. Before you leave the main highways for the winding mountain lanes, you can stop at a bustling travel stop, reminiscent of an American strip mall for road warriors. There, you might buy random knick-knacks, cups of instant sweet hot coffee, and snacks for the road. As you wander off the highways, the grey city erupts into brilliant green mountains. The air becomes cleaner as you climb the precipitous roads. There is nothing in view but lush trees above and rice fields below.

Approaching Sangju, you will drive past compounds of stark homes, built off the ground for protection from the monsoon season floods. Wander through one of these simple structures, and you will find a man so ancient that no one remembers his age. "He knew baby Soojung," a kind voice will tell you. He does not know you now—his eyes no longer see, for he is already of another world.

In an adjacent structure, larger now and full of young people, is the large, open-air kitchen where women prepare food while their babies play. The children will flock to you, for they somehow know you are different and curious.

You can unfold one of the low tables upon which you will lay out your lunch. You can retrieve all varieties of banchan from the bellies of sleek modern kimchi refrigerators, and within minutes a feast of bibimbap will be prepared. Perhaps you will take boxes of the region's treasured persimmons as gifts for your family back in Seoul.

If you wander behind the kitchen building, you will find the great clay pots, their patinas rich from the volumes of kimchi that has fermented within them and the generations of children who have played hide-and-seek between them.

It is a town that has not changed so much in fifty-five years, since Omma was born. To the north, Seoul has raced (palli! palli!) toward and boasted at the head of the world's economic table. But here in the heart of the Korean peninsula, Sangju has quietly held her many children, buried her deepest secrets, and healed her silver scars.

At the heart of Sangju, you will discover a grove of white mulberry trees on the side of a mountain. Hidden behind this grove, you will arrive at three large mounds— the graves of my ancestors. Their bodies feed the earth, which in turn nourishes the trees that provide sweet white fruit for the silkworms that feed the town's economy.

In the center lies my *harabeoji*, grandfather, who at one time was a prosperous shopkeeper and trusted bookkeeper to others in the trade. To the left lies his first wife, my halmoni, who nursed Omma at her breast and took our family's prosperity and optimism to her grave. To the right lies his second wife, who dedicated her mothering years to growing only unhappiness, who turned away a desperate, starving young mother and child.

*****

I have no idea what is going on. Hyunjung only tells me that we're going to the country to visit our grandparents' graves, so I plan for a daytrip. I'm not even sure what time we're leaving, so I wait on standby, feeling useless while everyone else scurries about. Appa packs coolers with food while Omma and Older Imo fill many bags with pots and dishes. Younger Imo arrives with her husband. As the activity increases, I see that everyone has packed overnight bags.

"Hyunjung! Are we staying the night? Do I need to bring something?" I ask.

"Ah, yes we are staying at a house. You should bring some clothes."

Hyunjung has been a great many things to me—new friend, confidant, translator—but right now she's failing me as a tour guide. I rush back to Omma's bedroom where my suitcase lives. I don't have a proper overnight bag, so I throw some essentials into a grocery sack. Although I've been sitting around doing nothing all day, now I'm in a slight panic as I try to quickly pack.

Omma shoves us out the door. I want to be helpful, but everyone pushes me aside without a word. I ride the elevator down to the ground floor and walk outside where the cars are waiting. Since no one lets me help, I just wait to take orders.

Eventually, someone points me in the direction of Appa's white Daewoo sedan. As I approach, I notice that there are already five others aboard. Surely I'm not supposed to climb in too? But yes, without regard for seatbelts or maximum capacities, I am told to wedge myself in between Hyunjung and Omma. Of course, next to Omma, always next to Omma. She has not loosened her grip since we met at Incheon airport.

Then we're off, cruising away from urban Hwaseong to increasingly rural vistas. We have two cars packed full: me, Omma, Appa, Older Imo, Younger Imo, Uncle, Hyunjung, Hyunsik with his wife and daughter, Eunjin with her son, and both of Young's daughters. Two very hot, squishy, cramped hours later, we climb out of the car at the home of some relatives in a town called Sangju.

Within minutes we gather around the low bapsang tables for a lunch extravaganza. We construct great bowls of bibimbap—piles of white rice mixed with various banchan, kimchi, savory-sweet *gochujang* pepper paste, and neat sheets of seaweed *gim*. Just a little lunch for us.

In a flash, lunch is cleared and we are loaded back into the cars, making our way across a small bridge and then climbing a winding mountain road. Our destination is a circular red-earth home on the side of the mountain, and the family makes quick work of unloading the contents of both cars.

I've never seen a house like this. As I approach from the road, four wooden *jangseung* totems greet me with their funny faces that offer protection from evil. I step into the entryway, where low shelves are built to hold our shoes. Immediately inside the entry, I step into a large round room about forty feet in diameter. It is red earth inside and out, to promote spiritual balance and bodily health. The only furniture in the entire building is one small, low bapsang table. Attached to the round room at my front is the kitchen, at my left is a bedroom with no bed, and at my right another bedroom, again with no bed. Overhead is a large loft.

I have no time to linger. Older Imo rushes me out, and Hyunjung tells me it's time to visit the graves of our grandparents now. The group is cheerful and chatty as we trek up the mountain, through a grove of mulberry trees, and on to three grassy mounds. We tamp down waist-tall weeds so that Younger Imo and Uncle can unroll a blanket before the large mounds where my ancestors sleep. At the same time, Omma cuts a watermelon and distributes its juicy slices. We make a strange memorial to my eyes, with us stomping the ground and spitting seeds.

After we've eaten the watermelon, Older Imo removes her shoes and walks to the center of the blanket. Feet together, she lowers to her knees, and then bows her head and hands to the ground. She seems to be praying, or maybe just talking to her long-dead parents. I feel like a tourist in this solemn ceremony.

Next is Omma's turn, but instead of walking to the blanket alone, she takes my hand to join her. I'm stunned to be included in their tradition; I am a crude violation of this rite. As I kneel low and place my forehead to the ground, I wonder what Harabeoji and Halmeoni would think about this American bowing at their graves. I also wonder if my skinny jeans have ridden up and if I have a crack problem.

After everyone has taken their turn, we pack up our gear and return to the house. Omma clutches my hand as we walk. Once at the house, Eunjin and I rest on the floor of one of the bedrooms. We are exhausted from the long drive and afternoon in the grove.

"Omma never hold my hand. Even when me and Hyunsik small, she never hold our hands. You are different. Always, she holds your hand," Eunjin says.

I don't know how to respond. I want to apologize for stealing that small part of her childhood away from her. For so long I've only dwelt on my own loss, not understanding how many others have suffered because of my absence. When a family loses a child, they lose a part of their heart, and now that I'm back I don't know how to return those broken pieces.

Eunjin doesn't seem melancholy about it though. She is content now—glad to have a new sister, glad to see a new, vast happiness in our Omma. She continues chatting in her rudimentary English, telling me about her husband, their home in Yongsan, some things about Jooeun, her son.

*****

It's never long between meals with this family; you

never have a chance to get hungry again before they are serving the next masterpiece. The kitchen is already bustling with dinner preparations—sliced pork belly, savory sauces, banchan, and a variety of lettuce leaves that Omma and Younger Imo have gathered from a nearby garden. Someone lays several blankets out beside the house, near the charcoal grills. Someone else lights the coals and begins grilling samgyeopsal, pork belly. We sit on blankets and dine.

A car loaded with three men arrives. The oldest is about Omma's age, old enough to be my father. He walks directly toward me, though I have no inkling of who he is. He walks quickly at first, but as he approaches, his steps slow to a shuffle. His eyes remain wide and fixed on me, and as he draws close I see that he has begun to tremble. He seems to age fifteen years on the path from his car to me.

I stand. He stops before me, and grief breaks over his face like thunder from a storm. Great lakes roll from his eyes, and down over his creased cheeks. He sobs and repeats my name over and over, "Soojung-ah, Soojung-ah, Soojung-ah…" He wraps his arms around me in a hug, even more distraught than Omma's first embrace had been. This old man whom I do not know holds me, rocks me, and cries my name, *Soojung-ah*.

Finally, after several long moments, he releases the embrace and takes a step backward, his hands still gripping my shoulders. Hyunjung's voice is at my shoulder, a whisper: *This is your uncle. This is your omma's older brother.*

Now I understand. He is the uncle who turned Omma away. He wanted to help Omma and her baby, wanted to take us in, but his wife had forbidden it. He did not know yet the lifetime of regret he'd endure from losing a child. I watch his face now and see these many complex emotions upon it: remorse, sorrow, and relief.

The two younger men approach now. They both speak some English, as many of the younger generation do. They introduce themselves, but there are too many new names and faces. I call them both *oppa*, or big brother. They hug me, and then they sit to eat.

Older Oppa can't stop smiling. I find him staring unabashedly at me, and when I catch him, he sits taller and grins more broadly. He positively beams. I don't understand his behavior; I wonder if I have *ssamjang* in my hair. After some time (and many Hite beers), Older Oppa returns to my side for another hug. He also seems to not want to let go.

"It is so good to see you, Soojung. I remember when you were a baby. We were young children together. I always wondered where you went. It's so good to see you again." Barely contained tears shine in his eyes.

Hyunjung's voice is at my shoulder again.

"We have not seen this uncle or these cousins for more than ten years. We are so happy to be together again. This is for you."

I realize now that this is a family reunion, and I am the reason for it. I'm awestruck by this circumstance, by how important every person in the world is, and by how many people even a baby can touch. How could I have ever thought that I was unimportant? That nobody missed me? Every person is so significant, sometimes even more so through their absence.

I understand all the ways this family tried to hold onto me—Omma, Imo and her husband, this uncle, my grandfather—but like vapor, I passed through their fingers. Am I any more real here than I was in Kentucky with my American family? They could not catch or hold me either. I am a spirit suspended between two worlds and two families, to be forever in between. I am a ghost of Sangju, of Seoul, of Shepherdsville, of St. Augustine. I am a memory keeper's daughter, made of lovely bones, child of Orleanna Price and Philomena Lee. I am every parent's worst nightmare and deepest fear: the missing child.

I am so sorry for all the pain I have brought to Eunjin, to this uncle, to so many people—but how can a ghost ever learn to do more than haunt?

Dinner drifts into talk and continuing cocktails of soju and Hite. Family drifts in and out of the house. Brett and my kids Facetime with Young's girls, and then Omma, Imo, and all the rest. My young niece says that she wants to come live with us because my children don't have to study too much. Newfound cousins in opposite hemispheres speak different languages and giggle at each other's faces. Every moment is a fresh miracle.

Uncle presents a photo that none of the sisters have ever seen, a sepia-toned photograph of their mother when she was young. Her face is extraordinary; even through the decades I can see her beauty, intelligence, and resolve. She died so young, and the loss of her tore Omma's family apart. I add her to my heart's collection of extraordinary grandmothers—Gran-Gran, Mamaw, and now Halmeoni.

It's time for *noraebang*, the Korean equivalent of karaoke, literally translated as "singing room." We gather our family and soju bottles in a large noraebang room down the hill from the red-earth house. Appa is jolly; his cheeks glow from soju, family, and singing. Omma takes her turn at the microphone, belting old Korean songs, her strong voice wavering in the traditional style. I wonder how Korean women make their voices like that.

Eunjin tells me, "Soojung! You must pick a song."

Omma pushes the thick songbook toward me.

"*Aniyo*," I reply—No. I don't sing in public.

"*An-i-yo. An-i-yo.*" Eunjin laughs, repeating my words. "It is funny. You say an-i-yo like child."

Her comment is not mean-spirited, and she doesn't realize how close she has hit to home. *I* am *like a child*, I think. *A child learning to talk, learning to live in this family.* I give in and select an American song that is fast but easy to sing. It's a song about being one big family, about our right to be loved.

After my turn is over, I watch them. This family is so comfortable together, singing, dancing, and sharing their lives as easily as oxygen. I've had too much to drink and I'm sentimental. I can't hold back the kind of thoughts that I'm ashamed of—thoughts of longing, of wishing. Childish and selfish thoughts that I turned off many years ago when I wanted to be a good, happy girl, when I transformed myself from Soojung to Raina.

My mind turns now to questions of how it could have been with this family, of how easy I could have felt, how right, how different I might have been if I didn't feel like a fake and a fraud all those years. I'm wracked with anger and regret that we didn't have a chance together. I admit that, no matter how well my life turned out in America, it might have been pretty great here too, and how neither my American nor Korean families are more worthy than the other. The unfairness of it all overcomes me, and I break into rolling sobs. My Korean family surrounds me, they tell me to be happy, that everything is okay now. They smile and want to move forward, but I just need a few moments to look back and grieve. I don't know how long the grieving will last, I wonder how it can ever end.

Omma walks with me outside—she wants to be my mother, to bring me comfort. We both have our dragons to slay, but in that moment we have a sweet, brief chance to just be a mom and daughter. She holds me, and though she has no English, she whispers through time, "You okay, Soojung.   You   okay."

Part 4
Reconciliation

"Healing may not be so much about getting better, as about letting go of everything that isn't you—all of the expectations, all of the beliefs—and becoming who you are."

~ Rachel Naomi Remen

Both of Me

Omma's letter, May 4, 2014

Time flew too fast, and on June 3, she went back to the USA. I went to the airport with her. Hyunjeong also came to the airport. My elder sister, Hyunjeong, Eunjin, and Soojung and I all had coffee together and took photos. I tried not to cry, as my daughter was going back to a happy life.

We said we will meet on October 1 and said goodbye with a smile. But when I came back home, I lost all my strength. I wanted just sleep, nothing else, but I could not do so. I cooked meals, did laundry, took and picked the grandchildren up from kindergarten, and I slept in all my spare time.

Soojung was with me all the time during the last thirty-four years, and now I had to send her away again. I could not understand why I felt so empty. Now Soojung had an American name, four children, and a husband in the USA. Sometimes I saw Soojung on Facebook, as my daughter showed me. Still now I could not believe this woman with an American name and Soojung are the same person. Where is my daughter Soojung? I have to see my daughter as Soojung from now on.

*****

This damn suitcase. I pull everything out of it and, for the third time, start over again with the folding and jamming like an ajumma cramming more kimchi into the pot. Everything has to fit—what else was the purpose of schlepping this half-empty monstrosity all the way to Korea if it can't hold everything I need to return with? Its empty half is failing me.

I survey the contents on Omma's bed. My personal

items have not changed in number, but the gifts I brought are now multiplied into dozens more that I will take away. The array is dizzying, and I use my phone's camera to document each gift, its giver, and its intended recipient. Trinkets from Omma, Appa, Older Imo, Younger Imo, Eunjin, Hyunsik, Hyunjung, intended for Brett, my parents, my children. Each present is to act as a bridge between my two families that are now, in this strange circumstance, becoming one.

The gifts are no problem, but it's the food that I can't work with. Besides the sheer quantity of it, there's also the size to deal with. Spread on the bed and overflowing to the floor, I assess my opponent: two cases of gim (dried seaweed sheets), a 400-count box of green tea, a Costco-sized case of instant coffee packets, packages of chocolate and strawberry Choco pies, bags of red ginseng, a package of traditional *kkultarae* (spun honey candies) from Insadong, and a case of frozen persimmons from Sangju.

If Omma can't keep her arms around me here, she will send me off with these bite-sized artifacts of her love.

I wrangle most of it into my suitcase and call it quits. Not everything will fit—it's time to cut inventory. I segregate the frozen persimmons (they were impractical for twenty hours of travel, anyway), one case of gim, and half the green tea. Then I shove everything else in and sit on top of my suitcase to zip it closed.

After a long drive from Hwaseong to Incheon, Omma, Imo, Eunjin, and Hyunjung are with me at the airport. I check in, heaving the cursed, blessed suitcase on the scales and breathing with relief that I am under the weight requirement.

We linger before our goodbyes. We drink sweet coffee and wade through long, heavy moments of silence. There is no right or easy way to end this trip, and we muddle through as well as we can. Again, like so many years ago when I first arrived in this country as a lonely, frightened young woman, I hate the airport.

This time, though, I hate it a little less. Although I'm leaving so much behind, I'm also returning to so much: my husband who has loved me through these times that I have been most unlovable, our children who somehow haven't figured out I'm actually not the World's Greatest Mom, and my parents who wait patiently to see how their little girl will come through all of this. Just as I was splintered in half thirty-three years ago, I feel it happening again. But this breaking is different—it is like the cracking and setting of a bone that healed badly the first time. It will get better now.

I can't wait to get home, where somehow I will learn to make both halves of me fit into one whole life for good.

*****

Anyone who's had a life-changing experience knows the strange feeling when you come out the other side. The first thing that changes is your name, even if no one but you can tell it. All your friends and family continue to call you the same as before, but the old name no longer fits because that person is gone. You are different today, it seems you should be called differently. But we usually don't change our names according to our feelings, no matter how poor the fit. You slide your new self into your old name like a hand into someone else's glove.

Another thing that changes is the light. Suddenly the world is dimmer, or brighter, or just slightly tinted. It might be that your vision is actually what changed, because again, no one else notices. After that, everything else seems to transform. The shifts are so small, so nearly imperceptible, that you're not quite sure if it's everything else that's different, or just you.

Of course, life is always changing, and every experience changes our life in its own way. The miracle of humanity is our ability to assimilate all those experiences, to adapt and expand without crumbling to pieces. Each day we live a new normal—some are just bigger than others.

That's how I returned to my life. I carried my new normal inside and maintained my composure outside. Questions were asked and answered. Emotions were packed away. The dimensions of my two halves settled inside me, and I adjusted to the dissonance.

Endless Wells

Omma's letter, May 4, 2014

On October 1, I took a flight to the USA. After a fourteen-hour flight, Jeesoo came to the airport to pick me up. We slept in a room in New Jersey with Jeesoo's friend. Then the next day, we went to Canada together. We saw Niagara Falls and other tourist sites, but my mind was with Soojung and waited until I could see her again. I spent fifteen days in New Jersey but could not think about anything apart from Soojung. On October 19, I took a flight for Jacksonville.

When I arrived at the Jacksonville Airport, Soojung was waiting with a boy. When I saw the boy, I became emotional with inexplicable feeling. I nearly fell down with tears. The boy was Cade. I had seen his photos before; he is the third child of Soojung. I hugged him with all my heart. On the way to her house, I stopped by a Korean-mart and bought various Korean foods that Soojung likes. She likes Korean foods and eats so well. I met her adoptive parents; it was such good meeting. I went with them to a baseball game and tourist places. It felt like a dream. Two nights and three days was such a short time to see my daughter. I was so sad coming back to Korea.

*****

Autumn 2013

I sit at the kitchen table with my youngest son, Cade, as he carefully draws the unfamiliar shapes of hangul letters on the outside of a homemade envelope. I look up translations in an online dictionary and show him how to create the symbols. We admire his work together.

to: 한국나측

from: 캐이드

사랑ㅎ해요

to: Korean family
from: Cade
I love you

Inside the envelope, we place his hand-drawn card as the first gift he will hand to his new halmeoni. It's almost time to leave for the airport.

Seeing that I'm ready to leave, Mom and Dad gather up their belongings—hats, purses, small dogs. They arrived a couple days earlier to meet my Korean relatives who are visiting for a long weekend, and I think they want to get some rest at their hotel before dinner.

"Welp, alrighty then, sugar," Dad says. "We'll get goin'. Y'all have a good night and we'll see ya in the mornin'."

"What are you talking about, Dad?" I ask. "I told you we're having dinner here. You're coming back, right?" I look at Mom, demanding an affirmative response.

"Well, hon, we don't want to get in the way. You're gonna want to catch up with your mom and all," Mom says uncertainly.

You've got to be kidding me, I think to myself. I invited you to come all the way down here for a reunion, not to sit in a hotel.

"Are you serious? Catch up? We don't even speak the same language, what the hell are we going to do? We'll end up just staring at each other. You have to come back. I really want you here."

They exchange an insecure glance. Mom clutches her purse as if it will assure her that I am sincere, but it offers no solution. "Well, if you think it's really okay. We don't want to be in the way."

"Oh for crying out loud, Mom! You being here is the whole point! I asked you to come; I want you here. How can you be in the way?"

I wonder when we became like this—me the dominant daughter, them the insecure parents. I wonder if it's a natural rebalancing as children grow into adults, or if it's the imbalance caused by having both sets of parents back in my life.

"Well, okay then sugar. If you're sure it's okay." Dad promises they'll be back by dinnertime.

Relieved, I move on with my morning. Cade and I make the forty-five-minute drive to the Jacksonville airport and wait in the arrivals area. We check the information monitors just in time to see that the direct flight from Newark has arrived as scheduled. We watch and wait.

Jacksonville airport is a small, un-crowded airport. The arrivals gate is a long, straight corridor, but access is limited. As a result, you see your traveling party long before you can touch them. That is how Cade and I first see them, as if they are materializing from a dream. They first start out as shapes, dark-haired figures at the other end of a tunnel, tiny in comparison to the larger Americans around them. Soon, the shapes evolve into motion as I can make out the distinct, brisk steps of their gaits. Finally, their faces emerge—Omma, Older Imo, Jeesoo—and they are my family. Cade patiently grips his handmade card.

Omma approaches us and drops to her knees. She wraps her arms around Cade in the same type of hug I had received in Incheon—desperately grasping not just the physical body but trying to embrace the whole being. She holds his round face between her hands and gives him kisses. She laughs and cries at the beauty of him. Cade accepts all this affection with a shy grin and presents their card. *To Korean family, I love you.*

We collect their luggage and return to the car, where Jeesoo asks if there is a food market. I explain about our grocery stores, not understanding her question.

"Aunt wants to cook for you," Jeesoo explains patiently.

Yes, of course. Always feeding me her love, filling me with the country that I have been deprived of. We stop at Costco for a couple things, then visit two Asian markets that do not have the ingredients that Omma requires. By this time I'm exhausted from driving and reuniting, but I understand Omma's determination and make a last effort at a market I find on Yelp.

We pull into the parking lot, where the market signage is in Korean. This is promising. As I park, I notice the other shops in the strip mall. I silently hope that if Omma can read the two words in English "gentleman" and "club," she doesn't understand their meaning together.

Inside, however, we find an extravaganza. Omma and Imo pile their small shopping carts high, and we finally make our way home.

We aren't in my house five minutes, we haven't even begun to put away luggage and groceries, when Omma and Imo march into the kitchen and take charge. They neither ask for permission nor wait for instruction—the kitchen is an ajumma's territory, and woe to anyone who stands in her way.

Omma swiftly removes ingredients from shopping bags: fish sauce, gochugaru pepper powder, rock salt, chili peppers, silken tofu, sesame oil, sesame seeds, *jeon* pancake mix. Imo retrieves cutting boards, bowls, platters, and knives as if she knows their locations by instinct. Together, they make quick work of the vegetables: cubed napa cabbage and julienned daikon radish for kimchi, sectioned and quartered cucumbers for oi sobagi, ribbons of Korean chives for everything. I blink and the countertop is stacked high with vats of fermenting vegetables. In two hours, the kitchen is full and ready: japchae, kimbap, kimchi paejeon, oi sobagi, bibimbap. They are efficient and indomitable.

My parents return and I make quick introductions, *Mom meet Omma, Omma meet Mom.* In an instant, all activity screeches to a halt as we all watch these two mothers finally meet. They pause for a moment, taking each other in, each considering just how great the other woman's contributions have been. Here is Omma, the woman who gave up a child. Here is Mom, the woman who kept that child safe and loved. They have been ghosts to each other, each living on opposite sides of the looking glass, wondering and praying for one another for so long.

They embrace and dissolve into tears. They can't stop thanking each other, hugging, re-hugging, re-thanking, weeping. These scenes of hugging, clinging, and sobbing have become commonplace in my world now. This is how we heal.

Soon the gifts come out. Omma has loaded her suitcases with T-shirts (I love Korea!), socks (PSY, Shin Ramyun, funny monsters, men and women in hanbok), and of course, more food. After Omma presents her gifts, Mom brings out the old photo albums. She takes Omma on a picture history of my life. In the same way that Kim and I had met, the same way Malia and Maia had met, now Mom and Omma meet: as new sisters. They point at photos and laugh; they exchange stories. They chat in different languages, as if they can understand each other through their bond of mothering the same child. Translation is not necessary.

*****

The next morning, Omma wants to know when Mom and Dad will visit again. With Jeesoo as my translator, I tell her that they will return for lunch, and then we'll all go to Cade's T-ball game. She understands. She waits.

Shortly after noon, Omma brings me a large, flat box. This time, I recognize the shape and I already understand what the contents will be. This is my hanbok, the one we had ordered in Dongdaemun market. Again, Omma wraps me in these brilliant silks, only this time we are in my house, in my country, and it is my hanbok. She had brought a bit of her lost daughter to Korea, now I am bringing some of my lost mother and country to America.

The chima is a long, full crimson color. The jeogori is crisp white with a long, deep-blue otgoreum like Omma's. Omma struggles to pin my shoulder-length hair up. Then we are ready, only I don't know what we are ready for. I eat lunch in my hanbok. I wait.

When my parents arrive, Omma springs to action. Whatever we're waiting for, the time has clearly come. Omma greets my parents at the door, grasps their hands and positions them in my living room. They are also confused. She pulls me to her side, and together we stand in front of my parents. Omma lowers her knees to the floor and gestures me to do the same. Now I understand, and I feel a little mortified.

Omma and I raise the backs of our hands to our foreheads, palms forward, and then lower both our hands and our foreheads to the floor. Together we bow low three times, and between each, Omma gives her thanks.

Komapseumnida…kamsahamnida…komapseumnida.

I pantomime the motions with Omma, while every part of me rebels against this awful act of contrition. I fight my inner battle—my desire to stand up in defiance and independence rails against my desire to honor Omma's wish to thank the people who raised the daughter she wanted so desperately to keep. It's all so difficult.

Mom clutches her heart, and Dad removes his glasses to wipe tears from his eyes. It seems that Mom, Dad, and

Omma can never weep enough to express these multitudes of sorrow, joy, and gratitude. They are endless wells.

I have a photo from later that day of me with both my mothers. On my right, Omma wears large round sunglasses and the ubiquitous Asian visor, the kind that extends five inches from her head all the way around the sides. It is white with purple gingham trim and perfectly matches her polyester outfit. She is all purples and whites. On my left, Mom wears smaller-framed sunglasses and a large straw hat with orange and black feathers radiating all the way around the crown. Her hat perfectly matches her bright orange T-shirt that proudly declares, "This is my GRANDMA costume." These are my moms from opposite worlds, who have lived such dramatically different lives, and yet they both instinctively know that it's crazy hat day.

*****

Another day, another airport, another flight between the United States and Korea. It seems we've just welcomed them here, and already we are saying our goodbyes: me, Cade, Omma, Imo, and Jeesoo. Just as we had done a few months earlier in Incheon, we drink coffee and wait for another flight that separates us from each other.

Jeesoo makes blowfish and monkey faces at Cade, who has fallen in familial love with her.

"*Wansungee*," she teases him—you are a monkey!

"Ty is *geobugi*," I reply. Ty is a turtle.

"*Gundengi*!" Cade laughs, repeating his new favorite word.

The time has come, and we walk to the security gate where we make our final hugs. None of us know when we'll see each other again, so we avoid talking about the future. Just as quickly as they had reentered my life, they are gone.

*****

Summer 2014

Stories never really end, only the telling of them does. I'm still living this one, and I find that every day I have a moment when all the air goes out of me. During that exhale, the memories and emotions of these experiences flood me, and I'm so full with a flash of anguish that I'm not sure I have the strength to pull in oxygen ever again.

Then that moment passes and another arrives. In that next moment, I think of my Omma who chooses to keep breathing, and my children who have so much exhilarating breath ahead of them, and suddenly my lungs fill again. Every day: exhale grief, inhale joy.

Over the past year, Omma has joined the Dandelions, a support group of mothers who gave their children up for adoption. She speaks out against Korea's social injustice against single mothers. A national Korean newspaper runs a story about our reunion: "She had lived cold and harsh times when nobody would even give her a sip of water. Now the economy is better, but the support to single mother is still not enough. She points out the society should support families staying together instead of being separated."

In May, I receive the letter from Omma that explains the whole story of my father and the circumstances of my birth. She is no longer ashamed, and though she is afraid of hurting me with the truth, she can no longer hide it.

In July, Mom comes to visit. It's a typical visit in this new *after* era. There is still an uncertainty between us, not because anything in the past has changed, but because everything in the past is now known.

We talk about Omma.

"They say I'm like her, Mom. The cousins tell me I'm smart like she has always been."

Mom thinks carefully about her response. "Well, I don't know. I didn't really think y'all are too much alike. It seems like you're so much smarter than she was."

"Why do you say that?"

"Well, I just think you'd make better decisions than she did. You know, how she wanted to go back to that man."

I feel a defensiveness for Omma swelling, and an anger toward Mom.

"You think that was a choice Mom? You think in those circumstances you'd be able to do better or that I would? How can we know what we'd do? She's survived things we can't even imagine."

"Oh honey. I didn't mean that she's not smart. It's just that you… " Mom stumbles on her words. "I don't know, maybe you are like her, and maybe I just don't want to see it."

I'm stunned. Why wouldn't she want to see that I'm like the woman who is my Korean mother? Mom has had the privilege of being surrounded her whole life by people who she is like—why would she want to take that away from me?

And then I realize that she wants me to be like her. That, despite her open heart and show of support through the past couple years, she has fought with her own struggles. They aren't battles that I can feel responsible for, or that I can ease for her. But I can respect them, as much as she has respected mine.

I want to tell her she has nothing to be afraid of, that I'm learning how to love. That, just as my heart expanded to hold each new child, it can also expand to hold each new mother, sister, brother, aunt, uncle, and cousin. My heart can hold a family in America and a family in

Korea—it doesn't mean there is less space for each, but that there is more space for me. That's all she's ever wanted, to help me find my space, to know I'm loved, to give me happiness.

As I have seen my children, I now see her: not only as the woman sitting across from me, but as every woman she has ever been. In the lines of her face, I watch the years unfold. There is the first meal she fed to her terrified new child, a Kentucky twist on white rice drowning in sugar, butter, and milk. Repeatedly watching that child eat until she vomited, a child who couldn't comprehend the limitless bounty of America. There is the cool of her voice reminding me that I am not ugly, that Oriental women are considered the most beautiful in the world, not realizing I have no reference besides the awkward, chubby-faced child in my mirror. There is the woman who knew nothing better than to pretend I was just like any other child in our community, who was taught that ignoring the pain, loss, and difference was the only way to manage it, who desperately and impossibly hoped to fill the gaping holes in my history and my heart.

My mind's eye watches an imagined movie reel of all the ways we've tried to be right for each other, and then all the ways we have failed each other. I could not achieve the happiness she needed me to find, and she failed to be the Korean mother that I had made my first, most formative attachments to.

It occurs to me now that I've spent so much of my life breaking her heart, and she has always tried to answer with a love that I struggle to accept. It is a flawed, incomplete love from a woman who adores a daughter she can't understand. It is a blind love that needs to believe in the goodness of her adoptive motherhood and hope for her melancholy child, and therefore found assimilation a greater virtue than identification. It is a pure love that couldn't see, understand, or repair the many things that convinced me of my unworthiness.

Am I worthy now?—In fact, was I ever *un*worthy? I've wasted so many years reaching for some identity that suits what I think other people wanted or needed me to be, thereby earning their love and justifying my existence. I see now that I've always deserved to be loved, to have a family and a home—because these are things that no one has to earn. They are all of our birthrights. We are all worthy.

The divide between the known and unknown halves of my life prevented me from claiming those rights, but now that divide is gone. The only division I face now is that of the known past and unknown future, and the future requires forgiveness and acceptance.

I forgive Mom for not being a mother she never could have been and accept her for the mother she was. For all the things she could never give me, such as a way to be comfortable in my skin, or an identity that soaked all the way through me, or how to reconcile a love that abandons with a love that holds fast. I forgive Omma her hard life and mistakes that led to our many years apart. For all the ways she broke her own heart, and the heartache I shared from half a world away. This forgiveness is not for their sake—no, neither need my forgiveness, for who am I to absolve them? It is for my own sake, so I can let go of my shackles and move forward.

Most importantly, I accept myself and my worthiness. After all, I know the truth now: Omma did not abandon me. Now I have two mothers who would die for me and four children for whom I would in turn give my life.

Is that enough to sate this soul? Can a starving child ever be full?

I am inexorably greedy for that which I'm just learning to accept.

Closing

Omma's letter, May 4, 2014

February 15, 2014 was Soojung's birthday. I got up early and cooked seaweed soup with japchae. I had cooked seaweed soup every single year, but this year was more meaningful. I took a photo of the seaweed soup and sent it to her, saying, "Happy birthday to you!"

Although I met her joyfully, how can I understand all her pain and fear?

But I never forgot you, even for one second in my life.

My daughter Soojung, I am so sorry as a mom.

Acknowledgements

This book was in work long before I started writing it. I have many thanks to give:

First, to Kevin Vollmers and Adam Chau, who read a couple of poorly written chapters and saw the potential for a spark—you took a chance that something beautiful would come out the other side. Indeed, it would not be nearly the book it has become without your gentle corrections and counseling.

To Erika Fisher, Shelise Gieseke, and Julie Koch who made sure all the words and punctuation were in the right places. To Kim Jackson who made us a beautiful cover.

To Julie Stromberg who brought it home.

To my early advisors, Joan Romano, Laurie MacDonald, and Kristina Adent. You gave me the cheerleading and confidence to keep writing.

To my beta readers and reviewers (so far): Cathy Loughman, Elizabeth Olsen, Michelle Clendening, Mila Konomos, Lee Herrick, JaeRan Kim, Randy Reyes, April Dinwoodie, Laura Dennis, Maureen Evans, Grace Newton, Koji Sakai, Deanna Shrodes, and Philomena Anne.

To my American parents and extended family, for your generous hearts and courage.

To Omma and my Korean family, for never forgetting a child you lost long ago, and for never giving up hope. I will never be able to properly express my expansive gratitude for returning to me a truth I thought had been forever stolen. Your story—our story—is the most tragic and miraculous I have ever known.

Finally and most importantly, to my husband Brett and our four children. I know I'm hard to live with, that I rage in ways you can't understand, and that you got far more out of this relationship than you bargained for. Because you love me through all my evolutions and accept me through this crazy, extraordinary adventure: my heart explodes with thankfulness. I'd be lost without you.